AF673525

MANAGERIAL EFFECTIVENESS:
Indian Insights

MANAGERIAL EFFECTIVENESS:

INDIAN INSIGHTS

Edited by
Sunil Kumar

EXCEL BOOKS

SRI SRINGERI SHARADA INSTITUTE OF MANAGEMENT
VIVEKANANDA CENTRE FOR HOLISTIC MANAGEMENT

ISBN 81-7446-112-4

9 788174 461124

First Edition: New Delhi, 1998

Copyright © 1998, Sri Sringeri Sharada Institute of Management
All Rights Reserved.

Published by
EXCEL BOOKS
A-45 Naraina, Phase I,
New Delhi - 110 028, INDIA
in association with
Sri Sringeri Sharada Institute of Management
Shankra Vidya Kendra, Paschimi Marg, Vasant Vihar, New Delhi-110 057
Tel.: 6140171, 6140589, 6140597
Vivekananda Centre for Holistic Management
14, Palam Marg, Vasant Vihar, New Delhi-110 057
Tel. : 6141173, 6148972

Printed at
BABA BARKHANATH PRINTERS
NEW DELHI - 110 015

Benedictions

H.H. Shri Bharti Tirtha Mahaswamiji The Jagadguru of Sringeri

A man in charge of an institution must have the ability to lead without swerving from Truth.

The manager must have special fortitude and enthusiasm for the job. Even if he succeeds very well, he should not feel proud or haughty. He should also be merciful. The people working for him must be really pleased with him.

The great poet Kalidasa, in his *Raghuvamsa,* describes the manner in which Aja Maharaja administered his kingdom.

"Ahameva mato mahipateh iti sarvaha prakrutishwa chintayat"

The poet says: "The king's behaviour was such that each of his subjects thought that he alone was very dear or close to the king." If a manager has this quality, the organisation will run most satisfactorily.

The manager should also have the definite realisation that, while he does his job scrupulously well, the result of his endeavour is according to *Isvara sankalpa,* or dispensation of the Lord.

"Muktasangoanahamvadi drutyutsahasamanvitaha Siddayasiddayornirvikaraha kartasatvika uchyate"

The *Bhagavad Gita* sums it up very well: "Liberated from attachment, not uttering 'I', endowed with the power to sustain and enthuse, unaffected in fulfilment or failure, such an actor is said to be *sattavic.*"

From *Tatvaloka* in its Issue on Management in the *Shastras,* based on the First National Conference on Indian ethos in Management.

Preface

This book is a compilation of articles and lectures delivered by eminent Management Gurus during various conferences on Indian Ethos in Management, organised by Shankara Vidya Kendra, Vidya Bharati Foundation and Vivekananda Centre for Holistic Management, over the last decade, under the leadership of Dr. M.B. Athreya and coordinated by Prof. Sunil Kumar. The search has been to see how Indian Shastras, containing the universal values and spiritual wisdom of mankind, can help in producing value-based managers and enlightened leaders who can create the environment, systems and organisations where people work together in joy and happiness, offering their best for the good of society, not in competition and tension but in a spirit of cooperation and equanimity.

The Indian Shastras clearly bring out that work is not just for *roti, kapada, makan* but it is also our opportunity to grow towards infinite perfection and joy. It is the educated people, the corporate leaders and the managers who are the *Shreshta,* the elite of the society. Whatever values and work ideals they as the *shreshta* practise will be followed by others. Therefore the need to know the highest and the best work ideals. Through these conferences we have learnt that Indian Shastras have a lot to contribute for Managerial processes like Human Resource Management, Leadership, Productivity, Motivation, Self development, Organisational Effectiveness, Corporate Governance etc. These have been the themes of our conferences held every year since 1989 in association with various organisations like the Indian Merchants Chamber, Mumbai; Prof. S.K. Chakraborty of IIM, Calcutta, the pioneer in value based management; IISc,

Bangalore and Management Associations of Ahmedabad, Chennai, Hyderabad, All India Management Association, New Delhi etc.

As a result of these interactions with a wide cross-section of corporate leaders and managers across the country, has emerged a group who have tried to evolve an Indian Management Model which can guarantee success because it is based on a harmonious blend of latest management thoughts with the time-tested eternal principles. Some case studies are also discussed in the book.

Secondly, a need has emerged for setting up a Management Institute with focus on Indian Shastras which could create the *Shreshta*, the elite, who would strive for achieving the highest and the best and thereby create the organisations which can produce and offer world class products and services, solve the problems of the people and make India once again a leader in the world affairs. With the blessings and support of HH The Jagadguru Shankaracharya of Sringeri Sharada Peetham, a new Management Institute with Focus on Indian Shastras has now come up, offering 2 years, full time Post Graduate Diploma in Business Management, approved by AICTE, Govt. of India, under the Sringeri Math, with the name of Sri Sringeri Sharada Institute of Management.

This book has been compiled in an effort to bring together at one place some of the basic principles of Indian ethos, its need and, its relevance to managerial processes. The first four chapters of the book bring forth insights from the *Upanishads*, Vivekananda, the *Gita* and the *Mahabharata* for leadership. After all, it is the managers and corporate leaders who are the real leaders of society today, because it is they who manage the vast workforce of the nation. It is necessary that they must be aware of Indian ethos and its ideals because it is the leaders whom the people will follow. Chapters 5 to 8 deal with the goal of life and self development and explain with precision the Indian worldview of "oneness" which is the uniqueness of Indian ethos in contrast to the worldview of "separatedness" which prevails today. It is only when we begin to appreciate the concept of oneness that our work and our managerial processes will take us on the critical path to the happiness that we really seek from all our activities. Chapter 9 from Dr. M B Athreya gives an overview of *Shastras* for modern management.

From Chapter 10 onwards we move towards applications of Indian ethos in Management. The necessity of Indian ethos is clearly brought out in Chapter 10 by Sw. Someshwarananda. Chapter 11 gives various insights and work ideals whereas Chapter 12 makes out a case for Vivekmanagement, i.e., managing through wisdom, instead of just management so that in and through excellence in our work we may also grow towards joy and happiness. Chapter 13 is titled Ethics in Management, but really, all articles in the book have the same purpose, i.e., to bring-in ethics in all aspects of corporate governance and management. The focus however is on change in the innermost nature of man through awakening his power of *Viveka*, discrimination between right and wrong and *Sadhana* (self development) and *Swadhyaya* (self study). It is not possible to become ethical through external rules and controls alone, unless there is an inner conviction, which this book hopes to give. In fact this subjective focus of attention, growth of the inner man, is another uniqueness of Indian ethos in contrast to the totally externally directed, objective focus of the modern age.

Chapter 14 and onwards explain how Indian values and work ideals can be applied and have been successfully applied for improved individual productivity and organisational effectiveness.

Having been intimately associated with the Vivekmanagement movement to bring Indian ethos in our education and managerial processes, as its Founder and co-ordinator, it is a privilege to present this bouquet of universal values and ideals to give to modern managers, a flavour of Indian wisdom so that in and through excellence in our work, we may grow and achieve the goal of life.

This book is dedicated to HH The Jagadguru Shankaracharya of Sringeri Sharada Peetham who in his infinite compassion keeps on empowering us and has allowed us the privilege to work on this ennobling task of making India once again a leader in world affairs.

– *Sunil Kumar*

CONTENTS

1

Leadership Values

*S.K. Chakraborty**

"UNDERSTANDING *Shastras*"

By way of introducing management in *shastras*, it is as well that a precise notion about the rather omnibus word *shastra*** be formed. Without immersing into the welter of details, Sri Aurobindo's interpretation of *shastra* is both deep and accurate enough. According to him *shastra* is not the sterile mass of inert routine suited to *tamasic* mind. Instead, it is a legacy of teaching springing from the experience, wisdom and intuition of a race about the art and ethic of life. Its aim is to offer guidance for right living and not immediate pleasure. Its rules of right conduct must first be observed in

---

* Prof. IIM, Calcutta and the pioneer in introducing value based Management.

** The two root words for *shastra* are: *shashan* and *trayate*. *Shashan* means rules, regulations, instructions, etc. *Trayate* means that which saves, protects, delivers, etc.

words regarding the 'shoulds' and 'should nots.' Then only the habit of self-control thrives, and the individual thereafter becomes capable of advancing to his real freedom of the spirit. And for this 'all *shastra* is built on a number of preparatory conditions, *dharamas*', says Aurobindo.

Yet again he declares, '. . . it is a means, not an end.' And as to how *shastra* relates both to the individual and the collectivity, Aurobindo clarifies thus:

> The *Shastra* is something impersonal to the individual, and that gives it its authority over the narrow personal law of its members but at the same time it is personal to the collectivity and is the outcome of its experience, its culture or its nature.

Thus, if effective leadership can be viewed as involving more of 'values for becoming', instead of just 'skills for doing', then this 'impersonal to the individual— personal to the collectivity' characteristic of the *shastras* seems to demand continuous reflection and integral assimilation by a true leader. Otherwise, the leader will always tend to be caught on the horns of a dilemma, preventing himself from taking sure-footed steps towards self-transformation. Even in Western management thinking today, people are no longer content to talk merely of 'organisational change', or even of 'organisational development. The new aspiration is for 'organisational transformation.' And to this we add: it is idle to speak of organisational transformation without individuals being transformed, especially the leader. What India now needs most is inspirational leadership which alone can transform. How can *shastras* help this endeavour?

"The source of *shastras* are the *shruti* "

Here *shruti* means the *Vedanta* or the *Upanishads,* barring the

Bhagavad Gita. The *shrutis* concern themselves with transcendent, eternal verities, beyond *desha* and *kala*— time and space. The *Upanishads* do not seem to deal directly with secular leadership roles. Yet through a profusion of dialogues, stories, analogies and enunciations the *Upanishdas* as a whole develop not only a concept but also realizable goal of self which seems to be absolutely universal and general. By that very reason it appears to devolve most of all upon leadership roles in all ages to strive for and manifest this Self — no matter in which context such roles are worked out. To sum up *shruti* concept of Self it is thus:

> In each individual there is a core or essence which is an independent perfect constant, characterised by unchanging self-existent *poornatwa* and *ananda*. It lies obscured and unfelt because of the mental and corporal egoistic superimpositions. By patient detachment if this layer be thinned or removed, the individual core Self and the Universal Self then come into immediate contact. All actions by the individual then become true and correct since they then are thereafter the expressions of the Omniscient Cosmic or Divine Will, or Self, or Intelligence, or Truth.

The *shrutis, Mahabharata, Ramayana* and similar other sources normally discuss the lives, duties decisions, etc., of the Kings in their attempt to translate the hightest psycho-philosophical principles into the secular-social context. Therefore we shall have to move on from kingship to the more ubiquitous contemporary roles of Managerial leadership. This transition has appeared to us to be not a particularly difficult task. As the leaders of the vast network of organisations, systems and workforce it is the Mangers, on whom is the responsibility to undertake the role of earlier kings, entrepreneur and teachers.

LEADERSHIP INSIGHTS FROM THE SHRUTI

In chapter 4 of the *Brihadranayaka Upanishad* (*BU*) The sage Yajnavalkya arrives in the court of the King Janaka. And in section I of the chapter a most interesting and illustrative sequence of penetrating questions and categorical answers are presented which are summarized below:

	Janaka's Question	Yajnavalkya's Answer
1.	What constitutes intelligence?	The organ of speech
2.	What constitutes dearness?	The vital force (*prana*)
3.	What constitutes the essence of truth?	The eye itself
4.	What constitutes infinity?	The (ear) directions alone
5.	What constitutes the essence of bliss?	The mind itself
6.	What constitutes stability?	The heart itself.

As elaborations to each answer, the sage repeats the same assertion and advice: each of the above six elements is verily the Supreme Brahman, and that each one is to be meditated upon as such. Now, the Supreme Brahman is but the Upanishadic phrase for cosmic or Universal Will or Consciousness or Intelligence, of which the individual Self is an identical counterpart. Thus *Brahmavidya* or Self-knowledge (both being the same) is presented as an integral, unifying process to be performed by meditating on each salient component of the human frame as *Brahman* itself. This transformation of one's vision of the otherwise mechanically-handled psycho-physical endowments is a requisite for their wholesome application. A sense of purity, transcendence and elevation is implicit in the advice to meditate on the ear, the tongue, etc., as *Brahman*. This seems to be the best rationale for such counselling to the King.

Moreover it is quite instructive to note too that after the delivery of each reply and its explanation, the King grasps the meaning clearly, and humbly offers a 'thousand cows and an elephant-like bull' to the sage. But every time the offer is made, Yajnavalkya repeats the same answer. 'My father believed that one should not accept (gifts from a pupil) without fully instructing (him).' It is this sublime character of the binary leader-counsellor combination which has perhaps been the underlying sustaining power and force of the much-misunderstood Indian civilization.

It appears to be rather remarkable that Yajnavalkya makes no mention of 'brain' (a neuro chemical network) in his responses, although mind, heart and *prana* are uttered. The modern mind-set which seems to swear by the 'brain-intellect-reason' troika as the foundation for leadership, may have here something serious to ponder because of its replacement by the 'heart-mind-*prana*' combination in the *BU*. And so far as this author's memory goes, none of the *Upanishads* possibly makes any reference to the brain or its equivalent, although *buddhi*, i.e., Intelligence (not intellect) occurs frequently.

It is just as well that reference to the *BU* has ended with mention about *buddhi* or intelligence. The *Katha Upanishad* (*KU*) has something very useful on this theme. Swami Gambhirananda's English translation of Shankaracharya's commentary on the *KU* has employed the word 'intellect' in verses I.iii.3 to I.iii.9 while rendering the Sanskrit term '*buddhi*.' In the chariot metaphor used in these verses, the intellect is conceived as the 'charioteer' while the mind as the 'bridle.' The verses (5 and 6 particularly) then draw a capital distinction between the functioning of intellect in collaboration (*yuktena*) with two contrasting states of the mind: 'the uncontrolled' and 'the restrained.' While the 'restrained mind-intellect' partnership yields mature and discriminating (i.e., refined, wholesome) choice and actions, the 'uncontrolled mind-intellect' pair produces turbulent and destructive choice or actions. Thus, in psychological parlance, intellect is an instrument, a tool. This is different from the casual intelligence or Self or Consciousness. Only when a controlled mind, is the same as 'pure mind,' becomes associated with intellect, does the individual attain the capacity to function with and for Intelligence.

The implication of this analysis, based on the *KU*, for leadership roles is clear: much before paying attention to the acquisition of skills, information and so on, the real task has to be to work *with* the mind *on* the mind *for* its refinement and coherence. Leaders with unruly minds will project/ create turbulent environments in their respective contexts. There is no dearth of examples of such leadership at the national and international platforms.

In the *Isha Upanishad* (*IU*), first and second verses outline two distinct paths for self-development. Verse 1 stressing upon the cultivation of an eye which sees all things as covered by the Lord and upon not coveting the wealth of others, aims at the individual who is ready to realize the Self through detachment. Verse 2 on the other hand recognizes the person who is not endowed with this bent of mind, and therefore has to live by performing *karma* or work. But how? As Shankaracharya later unravels the import of verse 8, the best way for the second person is then to blend *karma* with *vidya*, i.e., work with meditation. Clearly, the *IU*'s insistence on *vidya* or meditation bears total consistency with the *KU*'s mandate for restrained or controlled mind.

LEADERSHIP VALUES FROM THE SMRITIS: LAWS OF MANU

In the *Manu-smriti,* the most well-known among the Smriti texts, a few practical guidelines are given on 'The King.' The most striking theme in this chapter appears to be the detailed exposition of the science and art of punishment. For a student with grounding in modern sociology a review of this chapter is likely to suggest the conclusion that society in those times must have been so depraved and lawless as to call for such a brazen espousal of the role of punishment. The principal formulations in respect of punishment in this text are:

1. The lord created his own son Punishment for the King; punishment is the protector of all creatures.
2. Punishment is to be inflicted justly.
3. Punishment alone governs, protects and watches them in sleep.
4. If punishment is improperly inflicted without consideration, it destroys everything.
5. Without punishment of the guilty, the stronger would roast the weaker like fish on a spit.
6. The whole world is kept in order by punishment, for a guiltless man is hard to find.
7. One who inflicts punishment should discern well.
8. They declare that King to be just inflictor of punishment who is truthful, who acts after due consideration, who is wise, and who knows the respective value of virtue, pleasure and wealth (*dharma, kama and artha*).
9. Punishment possesses a very bright lustre, and is hard to be administered by men with unimproved minds.

10. By him who is pure and faithful to his promise, who acts according to the Institutes of the sacred law, who has good assistants and is wise, punishment can be justly inflicted.

The foregoing points have positive insights for leadership, but the sociologist's probable criticism, mentioned above, should first be cleared out of the way. True, there may not be Kings today. The swelling statute books of endless variety, enacted by the governments of countries all over the world, do not support the inference that modern societies are a whit less afflicted by human guilt and depravity. The most mature stand to adopt would therefore seem to be: whether societies are ruled by Kings and monarchs or by elected parliaments and senates, human weaknesses and frailities persist in the same spirit, although in their expression the forms may change and opportunities increase with time. Once this clarity is obtained, we may then turn to the value-imperatives for leadership roles, sharply focused in the context of punishment, in the *Manu-smriti.*

(a) 'Punishment ' is sanctified, sacralized by the imagery that it is 'Lord's son.' Much of the later injunctions of the King about the use of punishment could be traced to this personification.

(b) A family of cognate qualitative pre-conditions are appended to the application of punishment. Thus:

- inflict punishment justly
- proper infliction of punishment
- infliction of punishment after due consideration
- infliction of punishment with proper discernment
- truthfulness of the king

- wisdom of the king
- need for improved mind to afflict punishment
- purity (of mind)
- truthfulness
- good assistants, and
- wisdom.

This list of qualifying attributes for the transformational use of punishment are similar to the counsel given by Bhisma to Yudhisthira on the art of chastisement or *dandaniti* in the *Shantiparva* of the *Mahabharata*.

The king's role in the *Manu-smriti* is one of highest self-discipline and constant mental purity. Punishment, if needed at all, then becomes a legitimate derivative. And it becomes potent too—in terms of setting off or accelerating the process of reformation in the punished. Many elders today recall with awesome regard and reverence those very teachers in schools who were the most strict and used punishment in ample measure. Many also feel grateful in later years of life for the chastisement received which had turned their course of life upward. Why then is there such widespread skepticism about or avoidance of punishment? It is due to the lack amongst leaders of each and every attribute listed above. 'Physician, heal thyself,' goes the irreverent proverb. The severe prescription laid down by the *Manu-smriti* for the king:

> 'Day and night he must strenuously exert himself to conquer his senses; for he (alone) who has conquered his own senses, can keep his subjects in obedience.'

There is no stopping even at that. This text enjoins upon the king not only the mastery of the sciences of government and dialectics, of the theory of various trades and professions;

it also requires of him the 'knowledge of the supreme Soul.' It is in this very last requirement that there is a grand convergence of the *shrutis* and the *smritis*. What is the baseline, practical *sadhana* for Self-knowledge mandated by both? Control of one's senses. Thus, realization of the higher Self is prescribed for both the pure *brahma-vit* as well as the active ruler, based on the identical foundation of sense-control (*indriya nigraha*). Management of the senses, ruling over one's *indriyas* is a prerequisite for wise leadership roles. For, since the out-going tendencies habitually create a riot of confusion at the discursive level, one can neither acquire a transcendent and synthesizing insight into complicated problems; nor can one muster the sustaining power of unshakable inner conviction to clinch and stick to a course of action dictated by such insight.

Tagore has some very profound words on self-restraint in its role: "When we find our centre in our soul by the power of self-restraint, then all our isolated impressions reduce themselves to wisdom and all our thoughts and deeds unite themselves inseparably in an internal harmony."

Self-restraint has always been propounded as a fundamental value. Why? It enables recentering the de-centred, scattered consciousness. And since perfection and fore knowledge are already self-existent in the core of our being, recentering activates this core for spontaneous inner synthesis of all outer discordance. No leader can ignore such power in his search for the capability to inspire and hold together his human matrix.

Although the entire burden of transformation to bring back credibility in the use of punishment, in case of need, has been placed on the leader, reality must include team members also. The more the team members (subordinates being a dirty word!) are themselves indisciplined, self-centred or greedy, the more strident is their cry against authority, seniority and the like. If a leader takes a team member to task (privately) he immediately gangs up with similar other indisciplined shirkers or manipulators with sharp intellect. They together, often successfully, see to it that "bad money drives good money out of circulation." Humility, decorum are all thrown to the winds. How to be a good subordinate needs to be taught more than leadership: For, the good subordinate of today can be a good leader tomorrow. Obedience to the boss, even though painful, will always in the end, give a feeling of growth and expansion not contraction. The clue lies in the theory that the most enjoyable victory is over one's own lower ego.

The most relevant and arresting feature of the "collective personality of India" is that the secular has to be invested with and inspired by the sacred. The Raja Rishi is the Indian model of Leadership. It is a steady aspiration to live upto this Raja Rishi model which can save the severe credibility erosion in present leadership. Unlike the lower self-impure mind partnership now in vogue, the Raja Rishi model is built on the higher self, the Poorna core which can take healthy decisions.

All great undertakings are achieved through mighty obstacles.

2

Leadership in Management

*K.K. Chopra**

BASIC ISSUES

The subject involves discussion on two basic issues:

- What is Indian ethos and what are the characteristic values which project Indian ethos?
- What are the basic qualities which make a good and successful leader?

INDIAN ETHOS

Ethos is the habitual character and disposition of an individual, group or race. Indian ethos is essentially based on Vedantic philosopy—the oneness of the whole universe. One of the enduring fruits of *Vedanta* has been peace and harmony, tolerance and acceptance. This flows from its

* Former Senior Officer RBI and Secretary, UTI.

teaching of the non-duality of the ultimate reality and the possibility of different approaches to it.

Another important teaching of *Vedanta* is the innate Divinity of man.

Vedanta views the life of man in its wholeness. Its theme is Man—Man in search of fullness of truth, beauty and goodness. Part of this search is in the external world; but the most significant part of this search lies in the internal world; the first gives social welfare through the application of the physical and social sciences; the second gives spiritual freedom through the discipline of morality and religion.

Indian ethos has always emphasized moral and spiritual values as the foundation for human growth—both secular and spiritual. These values elevate the human personality to a level from where human beings deal with other human beings with love, affection equality, dignity and concern for their welfare. This character efficiency becomes a spring board for managerial effectiveness, resulting in better productivity, better house-keeping and better profitability in addition to a better and smooth human relationship.

EFFECTIVE LEADERSHIP

Man is always impressed by something extraordinary and great and is prepared to follow it if it touches his heart. If an honest of purpose and dynamic work efficient personality can be projected, then he can certainly sway the minds of people and make them loving and willing partners in all endeavours.

Leadership does not mean imposing will on unwilling, or submissive or unintelligent or docile persons working under one in an office or a factory. Leadership in social or service organisations means taking along people in the fulfilment of certain desired goals or set objectives. Leadership in this context is effective only through love, affection, sincerity, spirit of selfless service and by mutuality and cooperation.

Effective leadership can, therefore, be manifested by keeping this attitude in mind and building up personality and work efficiency accordingly. One must serve as a model for others in all respects, that is, honesty, integrity, hard work, dedication, courage of convictions, humility, fortitude, etc., and suffused with a humanistic impulse. When we are fortified by these values, leadership loses its sting of authoritarianism and becomes a source of joy and lovable inter-personal relationship. People become willing partners to achieve common objectives through excellent team-work, thus resulting in better efficiency, better productivity and better profitability and ushering in a new era of prosperity, success and general welfare.

The following points will be of great help in this regard:

Practice of Moral and Spiritual Values

Moral and spiritual values constitute an integrating principle in any society, primitive or advanced, like cement that holds together separate bricks so as to produce the integrated structure of a building. They help to hold together separate individuals in a social organism, which then ceases to be a mere collection of separate individuals, like the building which has ceased to be a pile of separate bricks.

Indian spiritual thought holds that all values are created by man from out of the depths of his personality through the intelligent manipulation of his material and social environment.

Ethical values find manifestation in the context of interaction between human beings in society. Ethics, therefore, is inseparable from the social context and *vice-versa*. This is what Indian thought calls *dharma*. The Mahabharata, therefore, defines *dharma* as 'that which holds together, that which sustains, all human beings': *dharnat dharmam ityahuh dharma dharayati prajah*.

This moral impulse finds expression in an outward movement of love and concern for the other man. This is well expressed in the great utterance of Jesus: 'Love thy neighbour as thyself.'

All ethical values are essentially spiritual values. They proceed from the trans-sensual dimension of the human personality. This dimension, which stimulates the *dharmika* or ethical sense, is beyond the reach of animals and of such humans also who, like animals, are content to live at the sensate level—*dharmena hina pasubhih samanah*, as the *Hitopadesa* pointedly expresses it.

Spiritual growth fosters and sweetens inter-human relationship as Lord Krishna tells in the *Gita* (III.11) '*parasparam bhavayantah sreyah param avapsatha*' (by mutuality and cooperation, all shall achieve the highest welfare).

What the nation has lost today is character and character is nothing else but an aggregate of moral and ethical values.

Work Efficiency

The *Chandogya Upanishad* written more than four thousand years ago, defines work efficiency:

> *yadeva vidya karoti, sraddhaya upanisada, tadeva viryavattram bhavati*

'Whatever work is done with *vidya* (knowledge) through *sraddha* (faith) and backed by *upanishad* (meditation) that alone become most effective.'

Mere theoretical knowledge is not enough. It is static; other parameters are necessary. What we need is a humanistic impulse, which alone can give a human response to a human situation.

Sraddha means faith, earnest belief, trust, loyalty, confidence, reverence, composure of mind and religious zeal. One has *sraddha* when one has a firm and active faith in the words of a competent spiritual guide and the revealed scriptures, and is ardent, earnest, and of set purpose. There is no room for frivolity, vacillation, scepticism, arrogance, pretence, and self-depreciation in a man possessing *sraddha*.

Courage of Convictions

One must have at least a few convictions if one wants to progress in life, influence people and achieve objectives. When one has convictions, one becomes a force. *Great convictions are the mothers of great deeds, said Swami Vivekananda.* One can change any situation or achieve any objective by developing tremendous convictions-political convictions, social convictions, moral convictions. It is always men and women with convictions who influence others. There are millions with opinions but very few with convictions. Opinions have no power to move the world, but convictions have. That is what we are lacking today.

Initiative and Drive

Electric energy locked up in the power house is of no use. It must flow through the cables and manifest itself through the medium of various gadgets so as to be beneficial. Similarly, passive goodness is never helpful. It has to be aggressive and vigorous and only then it can bear fruit. In other words, goodness has to be action oriented and result producing. Initiative and drive are, therefore, the essential prerequisites for effective leadership.

Sense of responsibility

We must accept full responsibility for the tasks assigned to us willingly and cheerfully. We can never discharge a responsibility effectively and efficiently if all the time we have the feeling that a particular work has been thrust upon us. Do not accept a responsibility if you honestly feel that you cannot discharge it. It is better to say "No" rather than to do the work half-heartedly. Responsibility about a task enjoins upon us to put our heart and soul into that work, with single-minded dedication, and devotion. We can never fail when we are determined to succeed.

Spirit of Selfless Service

Selfless service is the highest law of life. It prevails at the ethical and spiritual planes. It is given to the enlightened men alone to practice selfless service. The act of offering the best and the most useful in one for the welfare of others is selfless service or self-dedication. Both the giver and the receiver stand to gain through this sacred act. It is like draining the water away from a copious well into a fertile field. This bounteous act goes by the name of *Yajna* which literally means sacrifice. As fresh water springs out from an emptied well, the man who performs *Yajna* becomes more enlightened and prosperous.

Meritorious act untainted by selfishness, disinterested service, work of any kind performed for general welfare, adoration of the Almighty, ethical and spiritual endeavour—all these salutary activities are contained in *Yajna*.

Clear-cut and Worthy Goals

All actions must have a direction; otherwise, they lead nowhere. Quite often, there is a lot of movement in life but very little improvement or achievement. This is because there are no set goals, no planning how to achieve those goals, and thus always vacillating between different objectives and achieving practically nothing. So, one has to be very clear in mind about what to achieve, how to achieve and then reinforce it by a strong will-power.

Motivation

Need based motivation or monetary motivation in the shape of money, benefits, rewards, gifts, etc., makes a man mercenary and sometimes even worse. No human motivation can be generated and sustained for long by such inducements.

Effective motivation comes in as inner response from the stirring depths of the human spirit. I am a citizen of India. It is a proud privilege for me to be called upon to shoulder a great responsibility. This is the motivation that evokes the best from a person, provides a fillip to dedicate his life for the welfare of people and finally generates vast energies which are not only physical but mental, intellectual and spiritual as well. Therefore, one has to rise to a higher ethical and spiritual level, when alone motivation will become natural.

This type of motivation cannot be imposed or injected from outside. It essentially comes from within. It is indeed spiritual growth.

There are only two motivations which qualify for achieving greatness and make a person a true and beloved leader of the people. They are:

- Love of country, and
- Love of God.

Men, who have been influenced by these two motivations, have captured the hearts of people and have led them, not with the power of might but with the power of love.

This is the first lesson to learn: be determined not to curse anything outside, not to lay blame upon anyone outside, but be a man, stand up, lay the blame on yourself. You will find that is always true.

3

Managerial Leadership Dilemmas—Action Lessons from the *Gita*

*Dr. M. B. Athreya**

It is increasingly recognised that leadership styles, to be more effective, need to be rooted in the cultural ethos. Culture is a fabric woven with values, attitudes, models and habits. The Indian *shastras* are a repository of many such priceless ingredients of culture. The *Bhagavad Gita* has long been recognised as the essence of the Vedic and Upanishadic tradition. Its timeless relevance to the existential dilemmas of the citizen and the leader has been stressed by Adi Sankara in the ninth century; by Gokhale, Tilak, Aurobindo and Gandhi in modern India; by Max Muller, Matthew Arnold, Romain Rolland and others in the West. It is a scripture that

* Eminent Management Guru and leader of the movement for Indian ethos and values in Education and Management.

is going through newer contemporary editions and commentaries in several world languages. Here the focus is on the *Gita's* several guidelines for managerial leadership. The light of the *Gita* continues to reveal itself. So, this treatment is not exhaustive. It focuses on the first three chapters of the *Gita* which deal with Dilemmas, Knowledge and Action.

LEADERSHIP DILEMMAS

The modern manager faces many dilemmas. He sees many things tending to move in the wrong direction within and outside his organization. His recurring dilemma is—"To fight? Or, not to fight? The *vishada* of Arjuna in the very first Chapter of the *Gita* exemplifies this dilemma. Krishna's role in removing the *vishada* is a model of "counselling," which a manager:

- Should provide to his subordinate manager.
- Could receive from his boss manager.
- Having understood the *Gita,* need no more counselling for himself.

  Some of the dilemmas are—Should I allow—

  - the customer, dealer, supplier or shareholder to be exploited?
  - infringement of laws and regulations?
  - pollution of the environment?
  - manipulative politics within the organization?
  - unfair practices, by workmen, union or management?
  - sabotage of systems and procedures? etc.

Gita gives an unambiguous answer, Act. Do not feel helpless, afraid, pity, etc.

Shloka 1.1. Dharma Kshetra

As in the case of Kurukshetra, the modern Business Organization can be viewed as, a *dharma kshetra*. It is the role of leadership in reestablishing the *dharma* in all external and internal stakeholder relations.

Shloka 1.2. Acharya

As Sanjaya observes the battle scene, "*Raja*" Duryodhan first speaks to "*Acharya*" Drona. Similarly, the Manager, when facing a major issue, may discuss with his boss, Staff Officer or an advisor.

Shloka 1.3. Dhimatha Shishsya Bhava

Duryodhan refers to Drupada's son as a *shishya* of Drona who is *dhimatha* or *buddhiman*. The Manager may be more effective with power from knowledge, than from positional authority or control of funds. For this, he needs to be a life long *shishya*.

Shloka 1.4 to 1.9 Lakshanah

In role analysis in modern Human Resources Development models, the concept of "Critical Attributes" are required in the role occupant. In his leadership role, a manager will need the various attributes used by Duryodhan in describing even his enemies—

Sura	Courageous
Mahesvasa	Well Equipped
Viryavan	Determined

Nara Pungava	Outstanding among men
Vikranta	Victorious
Tyakta Jivitah	Willing to give one's life, if needed.
Visaradah	Highly competent.

Shloka 1.21. Nirikshan

Arjuna wants to take a good look at his enemies before beginning the fight. The Manager should not under-estimate his adversaries, but may love, respect and feel for them as Arjuna does.

Shlokas 1.28 to 1.30. Vishada

Arjuna eloquently describes his dilemma and expresses his feelings—Frozen limbs. Dry mouth. Shaking body. Hairs standing on end, Dropping of Weapon, burning, giddy, all symptoms of managerial stress, in different degrees!

Shlokas 1.31 to 1.43 Upavisan

Sitting Down/Withdrawal—Arjuna first declines to fight, despite so much injustice, suffering, *vanavasas*, *agnatavas*, etc. He gives several reasons—rationalisations?—Bad omens. No glory in this victory. Do not want victory, kingdom, enjoyment. How can I kill teachers, fathers, grandparents, sons, grandsons, in-laws, etc.? This violence may be sinful. Destruction of *kula* and *dharma*, etc. Rather let them kill me.

Arjuna's mind was heavily clouded with emotions. Managerial leaders also face such paralysing situations. They may be indecisive or take decisions of short-term convenience, but long-term institutional disaster. Has Arjuna thought of the consequences to the state, society and posterity of Duryodhan's victory, especially without a fight? No. Krishna reminds him. Teaches him. That teaching is relevant to every managerial leader. Arjuna learns that *rajya dharma* is more important than *kula dharma*. The manager needs to appreciate that *sangathan* (Institutional) *dharma* is more important than *vibhag* (Departmental) *dharma*.

Emotions like *kripa, karuna* have their place, but not towards those bent on institutional destruction. There is a lesson here on optimally "tough" management. There are no soft options for leaders. They are " trustees." They must take higher, difficult, irksome responsibility for fair resource allocation, objective appraisals, frank feedback, meritocracy, developmental transfers, exits, etc.

The path of knowledge

If disengagement under stress is a temptation for such a great, well trained warrior like Arjuna, it is quite understandable in a modern-day Chairman, Managing Director, Presidents, Directors, Vice-Presidents or General Manager. But Krishna's resounding, logical reply is helpful to all of us. It is no emotional appeal. It meets the manager's *prakriti* and grain for argumentation.

Shlokas 2.2 and 2.3 Uttishtha

Stand up and be counted—Krishna is not impressed by the noble Hamletian sentiments. He describes Arjuna's mental state in several words—

Kashmalam	Confusion
Vishama	Wrong timing (for otherwise right emotions)
Anaryam	Not befitting the elite.

Asvargyam	Not the way to heaven (including making a heaven on earth for one's people).
Akirtikaram	Bringing disrepute.
Klaibyam	Neuter gendering of self.
Hridaya daurbalyam	weakness of heart.

Krishna's advice is direct—

(a) *Tyaktva*—Give up the above unwise mental state.

(b) *Uttishtha*—Stand up (for battle).

The manager must realise that differences are not only inevitable, but desireable for better decisions. In exceptional cases, especially on value/*dharma* issues, he must fight to the finish, if necessary, to uphold the right corporate culture. Vivekananda has immortalised this message of the *Katha Upanishad* (I. iii. 14) in his call—"*Uttishtatha, Jagrata, Prapya Varan Nibodhata*" (arise, awake to your Self, and learn by approaching the excellent ones).

Shlokas 2.4 and 2.5. Pragya Vad

"Learned" Arguments—Arjuna articulates another salvo of arguments—fine human sentiments

Puja arhah	Deserving of my worship (Bhishma and Drona).
Gurun	Teachers (once my teacher, always one).
Mahanubhavan	Experienced, great men.
Bhaikshyam	Begging is better (for a simple life).
Rudhira Pradighan	Blood-stained victory.

The manager may occasionally have to differ from his superior; some other senior who once nurtured, counselled and developed him; dear colleagues with whom he has shared much fun—if they are on the wrong side of the institutional *dharma*.

Shloka 2.6. Avidya

Lack of knowledge, uncertainity—Arjuna expresses the classic uncertainty in all big decisions

(a) Who will win—we or they?

(b) Even if we forecast, we will win, should we defeat them?

Shloka 2.7. Shiksha

Seeking advice—Having experienced some catharsis, after giving free vent to his emotions, Arjuna cools down and seeks guidance, in all humility.

Svabhava	He realises his own nature, which is,
Karpanya	Full of mercy, which may some times be a,
Dosha	Weakness.
Dharma sammudah chetah	Mind clouded by confusion on what is right and wrong.

He wants to be advised, in a spirit of surrender as a learner, by his teacher on—

Yath shreyah	Which of the two alternatives is more reputable? He does not ask which is more profitable personally beneficial.

Shloka 2.8. Vishada

Doubt, again!—Despite the query, the doubt pierces through again.

Na prapasyami	I don't see how—even victory can overcome my—
Shokam	Grief, which is so high that—
Shoshanam indriyanam	Dries up my senses (with which only one enjoys life)

The Manager needs to check himself when he asks for advice, but is still not in a mood to listen to it; almost afraid that the advice may solve the problem, but he finds it unpleasant to implement the solution.

Shloka 2.9. Withdrawal

The grief and doubt still overwhelm Arjuna. According to Sanjaya, he ends his query with verbal and behavioural gestures of withdrawal.

No yothsya	I will not fight
Thushnim	Became quite. Shut up? Sulked?

Managerial dilemmas lead to similar symptoms of withdrawal, flight, procrastination, defiance, sulking or similar productive, ineffective responses. There are overt and hidden costs in such dysfunctional leadership behaviour to the team, the organization, and indeed, to the self.

Shloka 2.10. Prahasan

Smiling—When indecision is expressed in high flown language, the good teacher may experience anger, but tries to respond with a smile. That is what Krishna did. His philosophical reply is prefaced with gentle feedback.

Shloka 2.11. Misplaced Sympathy

Why regret for—

Ashochyan	Those who do not deserve sympathy (having, failed several tests of humanism).
Pragyavad	Making learned arguments (to justify that sympathy)

Managers also tend to make apparently impressive arguments to justify one's own inclinations. It is useful to become a —

Pandita	Knowledgeable person, going beyond one's function or role; especially knowledge of values and their impact on organization and society.

Krishna's detailed stress on the indestructibility of the soul is appropriate in its context, such as for leadership in the armed forces.

Shloka 2.31. Svadharma

One's duty—for a Kshatriya, it is war, when war is the inevitable last resort. For the managerial leader it is *shreshtha dharma*. His caste-based *dharma* may be followed in his personal life. In his official role, he has to uphold the *dharma* of the *shreshtha*, namely the elite, entrusted with resources and responsibility.This becomes all the more important in a world which has returned to the market economy.

Shloka 2.31. Yadhruchchaya

Chance opportunity—It is not often in a Kshatriya's life that a *dharmayuddha* comes. Arjuna should seize it. Similarly, the manager should seize not only new business opportunities, but also every opportunity to uphold institutional and societal *dharma*.

Shloka 2.34. Akirthi

Disrepute—Generations will speak poorly of Arjuna and the Pandavas for running away from a war against evil. Similarly, organizations have long memories. They remember good and bad Chairmen, Directors and other senior leaders. They may not say it to his face, but remember it. There is a feeling of being let down by him. Such *akirthi* must be particularly galling to the—

Sambhavitasya	Established, hitherto leader.

Shloka 2.35 Mamsyanthe

Perception—Opponents, and even warriors on your side, will perceive you as having run away from a just and necessary battle due to—

Bhaya	Fear—fright, panic? and
Laghavam	Being rather light—inconsequential, marginalised.

Organisational equations can change. Respect will shift from weak leaders to competent, value leaders. Although there may be fear, respect will not be given to leaders depraved like Duryodhan.

Shloka 2.36. Ninda

Abuse—People will abuse a shirker, particularly his—

Samarthyam	Competence.

A Manager should be known by his Self-Actualisation, in which contribution through one's leadership competence has a key role.

Shloka 2.37. Nishchayah

Decisiveness—Krishna asks Arjuna to rise with—

Krita nischhayah A mind made up to fight.

Many subordinates in modern organizations report that their own work, industrial relations, and the performance of the organization are affected by their leaders. Decision theory stresses the need to make a number of decisions, in order to improve the rate of success—the EMV, the Expected Money Value.

Shloka 2.38. Samatvam

Balance—Krishna advises Arjuna not be to calculative, but to do the right thing and accept with equanimity the results, whether—

Sukh, dukh Pleasure or pain

Labh, alabh Gain or loss

Jaya, ajaya Victory or defeat

This does not mean indifference. It is the most efficient behavioural strategy. Similarly, managerial leaders need to conserve their energy away from worry, but assess the situation, *dharmic* issues and act as best as they can. Their balance is likely to produce better results than their worry.

Shloka 2.39. Buddhi

Intelligence, Wisdom. Actions performed with true understanding will release one from—

Bandhan Bondage

Well understood and considered action will release the Manager from unintended, unanticipated effects. He will be better prepared to handle the predictable consequences.

Shloka 2.40. Kraman

Method—There is no wastage in good action. Methodical beginnings do not die or give contrary fruits. Even small acts of *dharma* can protect the Manager and his organization from—

Mahato bhayath Serious dangers

This requires a long-term perspective. Some managers tend to go for short-cuts at the risk of long-term profitability, growth, image and vitality of the business. The leaders need to caution them.

Shloka 2.41. Vyavasaya

Single-minded, decisive effort. True *Karma Yoga* requires a determined mind. The indecisive actor will see—

Bahu shakha Many branches (of the Decision Tree!) and

Anantah Never ending (branch and sub-branch lines).

Modern management theory advocates a DECISION TREE approach. All possible alternatives, their costs, pay offs and possibilities can be estimates and revised dynamically. But at each point, the Manager must take a Bayesian probability based EMV decision. Often, one sees confusion and circular indecision, but not a well laid out decision tree. It is amazing and thrilling to read the *Gita*, so early on, referring to *shakha's* or branches of *nischaya* (decision).

Shloka 2.45. Attributes

Some more leader attributes are brought out in this *Shloka*. *Nih trigunya*(or *gunatita*)—Beyond the three *gunas*, namely *sattva*, *rajas* and *tamas*.

Nir dvandvah	Without involvement in the emotions (of elation, grief, etc.)
Nitya satvastah	Staying at a *sattvic guna* level of behaviour, at all times.
Nir yogakshema	Not trying to appropriate and protect gains for oneself.

Shloka 2.47. Nishkama Karma

Work without attachment to results—This is perhaps the most relevant *shloka* and message for leaders in the practical world of affairs. In the modern era, this message is particularly apt for managerial leaders. But it is also the message which is most misunderstood by some. Due to an emotional over reaction, they fail to benefit from probably the most helpful message. It is important to understand the true meaning and importance of this *shloka*. It turns on the word—

Adhikar—

(a) Authority, control. Even in a strictly logical sense, is it not true that a manager has authority to plan, direct and guide *action* by himself and his team? But results are the net outcome of actions by self, others, environment, etc. If the mind is obsessed with the results, energy will be diverted from action. Through good action one can *influence* the results.

(b) The other confusion is about whether one has a "Right" to reward. In a legalistic, bureaucratic sense, yes. Here again, preoccupation with the right may reduce one's efficacy in action. Can one *trust* the superior, the team, the organization and the environment to give one the just rewards? Further, what is the manager looking at—

Short-term versus long-term rewards. Financial and social-psychological rewards. Esteem from others along with true self-esteem. Good standards set by others and one's own higher standards.

Anticipating the possible over reactions, Krishna also suggests that we avoid the temptation of

Akarmani Inaction

In summary, our submission is that nishkamakarma or unattached action is not a purely moral stance, but also the most efficient and effective strategy of action.

Shloka 2.48. Further Attributes

More leadership—Yogastah—Engaged in unattached action, by definition. *Sangamtyaktva*—Renouncing attachment, possessiveness—but certainly with involvement, trusteeship to serve. *Samah*—Equally at home with success and failure avoiding elation and complacency with success; avoiding depression and hopelessness with defeat.

Competition, seasonality, industry ups and downs and overall business cycles are bound to affect all managers. Can he be composed and direct his and organisational energies for a better response?

Shloka 2.49. Kripanah

The pathos of the calculative—The manager has the choice of being self-centred and bargain for rewards as a precondition of work. But is this the correct choice? It is a poor choice. A management scholar Amitai Etzion welcomes the move of modern organizations from "coercive" motivation to "utilitarian" motivation, but regrets failure in not strengthening "value" motivation. Managers objectify, alienate and de-humanise themselves and others by encouraging a predominant bargaining mode. This hampers Self-Actualisation, and even more dangerously, Self-Realisation.

Shloka 2.50. Kausalam

Skill, Excellence—In addition to *samatvam* (equanimity), *kausalam* is the second major definition of *yoga*. It is dexterity in action-whatever that action in one's role in organization and society. This stress on skill development once again helps remove the misconception of *nishkama karma* as resignation, fatalism, giving up, etc. No, *karma yoga*, blended with *buddhi* and *gnana* is interested in excellent results—first for the organization and as a result, for the individual.

Shloka 2.51 to 2.53

There are direct personal benefits to the Manager from unattachment.

Bandha vinirumkta	Released from bondages—the stress and strain, debris and residues of organisational rivalries, conflicts, tough decisions, etc.
Moha kalilam	Clarity brought to a mind clouded with a variety of ideas, forces and pressures.
Nishchala	Steadier mind, which is pushed in different directions by various, conflicting data and feedback.

Shloka 2.54. Sthita Prajna

Steadfast in Consciousness—Arjuna seems to be grasping

the essential model of leadership propounded by Krishna. He seeks clarifications on the attributes of this mental state—

Lakshan	What are his attributes?
Ka bhasha	What is his language?
Samadih	How does he carry himself?
Kim prabhashet	What does he utter?
Kim aasit	How does he sit?—Psychologically speaking?
Kim vrajet	How does he move about?

Shloka 2.55 to 2.61. Lakshana

The Attributes of *sthita prajna* are described by Krishna—

Atmana tushtah	At peace and pleased with himself—without looking for stimulation from outside.
An udvigna manah	Undisturbed by sorrow.
Vigata spruhah	Unattached in comfort.

Having overcome the emotions of—

Raga	Attachment
Bhaya	Fear, and
Krodha	Anger
Sneha	Affection
Kurma anga iva	Who controls his senses from sense objects, like a tortoise bringing its neck into its shell. This may appear rather hard.

But the higher up a managerial leader, it appears that he has to be a model of balance, discipline and appropriate austerity. He has to resist temptations of excessive ease, drink, food, sight-seeing, etc. He not only transcends the-*Vishayah*—the objects, but also *Rasa* the juice in them—There is no hankering and repression.

He realises that—

Indriyam	the senses can
Haranti	steal, distract, seduce the mind.

He does not need external control, but practices—

Samyama	Self-control

Shlokas 2.62 and 2.63. Atma Nash

Self-destruction—These two *shlokas* give one of the finest behavioural models of man seen anywhere in the behavioural sciences, literature, either Western and Eastern. The downward slide to destruction goes like a modern computer flow chart.

Vishayan	Man keeps thinking of sense objects.
Sangah	He develops attachment to them.

Kamah	Attachment leads to desire.
Krodh	When all object desires cannot be met, he gets angry (at the boss, peer, staff, organization or any such displaced target).
Sammohan	Anger generates intoxication.
Smriti vibramah	Loss/distortion of memory.
Buddhi Nash	Erosion of discrimination, judgement.
Pranashyati	Finally to self-destruction.

It is a tragedy of potential wasted due to lack of self-management. When a leader allows it to happen to himself, many others and the organization suffer.

Shloka 2.66. Positive Cycle

By implication, Krishna also suggests a positive cycle in this shloka—

Yukta	A self-controlled person gets—
Buddhi	More intelligent in his judgements, and
Bhavana	Positive, deeper values and attitudes in his *antah karna* inner working.
Shanti	That leads to peace—not in action, but a dynamic, robust, resilient peace,
Sukham	which can only give true pleasure—of contribution, institutional achievement.

Shloka 2.67. Charan

Drift—Opposite of "management." Krishna gives a beautiful analogy—

Vayuh navamiva ambhasi	As the wind drives a boat in water.

Should a manager drift with the winds? Or set a direction, strategy for his organization/team? How can he do that if he has no control of the lead boat, that is, himself?

Shloka 2.68. Summary

A further summary of leader qualities—

Nih spruhah	Unattached to rewards (but aiming at high performance).
Nir mamah	Unattached.
Nir Ahankara	Not egoistic.

THEORY OF ACTION IN CHAPTER 3

Along with the second chapter, the third chapter is relatively more relevant to the managerial leader. It is about—

Karma Yoga—the theory of committed, efficient, but unattached action. Is this a contradiction? Why? Peters and Peterman in their book "*In Search of Excellence*" talk about the need for "Simultaneous Loose—Tight Properties." Is it not a dialectic, with synthesis, rather than a contradiction? Or even better, a creative simultaneity of action and non-attachment. Why do we fear that non-attachment may reduce the vigour of action? Why does not the manager see that attachment can interfere with quality, spirit and mode of action?

Shloka 3.1. Escape Route

The desire to avoid unpleasant work is well-known to Managers. More time goes towards easier, pleasant, popular actions; and less time is available for difficult, but important, tasks-like counselling subordinates with negative feedback, pruning product lines or plants. Arjuna tries to trap Krishna with a counter-argument—

Karmanah te matha budhih	If you consider knowledge superior to action, why do you push me towards such terrible work, as the war.

He even accuses the counsellor, as subordinates often do.

Mohayasiiva	you are hypnotising me.

Also challenges Krishna to be decisive, clear—*ekam vada nischitya*—Tell me one thing for certain. Subordinates often cannot cope with ambiguity and will pressurise the boss to tell them things in black and white.

Shloka 3.5. Prakriti

The natural tendencies—Krishna responds to the need. He points out the simple reality that living creatures cannot be without some form of "work"—

Kaschit kshanamapi	Even for a moment. The *gunas* (qualities) bind them to work.

Shloka 3.6. Mithyachar

Misleading conduct—A leader needs to bring congruence between his "thoughts," on the one hand, and "words and deeds," on the other.

Indriyani samyamya	Mere control of the bodily actions will be like repressive behaviour, if
Manasa smaran	The dysfunctional ideas continue in the mind. In that case, he is
Mithyacharah	A trickster.

Shloka 3.8. Work Culture

Krishna is unequivocal that action (*karma*) is preferable to inaction. Managerial decision theory is clear that a series of decisions is generally better than indecision in a manager, in that even if some decisions go wrong, there is a statistical probability of net improvement. Action becomes superior if it is—

Niyatam	As prescribed.

In the organisational context, there are many corporate policies, systems and procedures, such as—

- GMP—Good Manufacturing Practices
- TQM—Total Quality Management
- CPM—Critical Path Method
- ABC—Pareto Analysis of Stores items
- VED—Pareto Analysis of Spares.
- HRD—Human Resources Development

These good concepts do not work well when there is "system indiscipline" at managerial and worker levels.

Shloka 3.9. Bandhanmukti

Bondage and liberation. How? The human condition is *karma bandhanah*—Bound in action.

This is true now, as we approach the 21st century, for individuals, firms, states and nations. The collapse of central planning in the biggest historical attempt in the Soviet Union indicates that no country can isolate itself and work less productively, or even allow pockets of inaction. So what is the way out?

Mukta sangah—To perform the action, without getting attached or possessive about it.

Shloka 3.10. Parasparam

Interdependence. Krishna also advocates action in mutual interest among human beings. The important thing is the "spirit" behind the action.

Parasparam bhavayantah	With the *bhava* or feeling of care and concern for each other.

Shloka 3.12. Offering

Krishna also emphasizes the need to offer. In the modern context, this would be—

- Offerings of the individual to his team;
- Offerings of the team to the organisation;
- Offerings of the organization to the society.

Those who enjoy

Apradya	Without offering or sharing, are no better than
Stena	Thieves.

The enterprise should give a fair deal to all its stakeholders—customers, dealers, suppliers, society, shareholders and employees. It should share the gains of growth and productivity all round.

Shloka 3.13. Residual Beneficiaries

As trustees, Manager may enjoy the residual portion of the wealth created by them, after distribution to the stakeholders. They will be like the *karmayogis,* who

Yajna shista ashinah	eat what is left after the offering (to gods, *guru* and guests).

Shloka 3.17. Self-Management

This stanza in the *Gita,* is again liable to be misconstrued. Krishna describes an individual with three attributes—

Atma ratih	Delights in himself. Has no feeling of inadequacy, inferiority, self-hate.
Atma triptah	Satisfied with himself, with what he has got, not in a complacent sense, but in a mature way, which releases his energy for future productive work.
Atma santushtah	Pleased with himself; not in need of much praise, confirmation, appreciation or what is known as "positive strokes" in Transactional Analysis.

For such a person, there is no

Karyam	Work, in the sense of obligatory tasks in order to get something in return, for which he craves.

This is not to be misunderstood as a prescription for idleness. In fact it may lead to purer, more efficient action, unhindered by a myriad of self-related anxieties. It is akin to, but goes beyond the "self-actualisation" stage of Maslow's hierarchy of needs.

Shloka 3.20. Janaka Model

The philosopher kings like Janaka, succeeded in life, which is more difficult than success in the battlefield, through work, which was aimed at—

Loka sangraham Public good.

Management has a social responsibility. Business leaders have to act for business growth and profitability, but in overall societal interest. So, corporate "image" is an important business objective—The onus on managements—

Sam pashyan By perceiving what is in the best social interest.

They should not wait for legislation, agitations and harangues by politicians.

Shloka 3.21. Role Model

This *Shloka* in a way summarises *Gita's* message for the modern elite, including Managers, who are now perceived, the world over, as part of the competitive advantage of a nation. There are no more Rajas (kings). What we have are *shreshthas*—the superiors, not by virtue of ascribed status, but by achieved/earned distinction in values, knowledge and skills. So, the modern leadership model may be called *'shreshtha dharma'* the duty of the superiors. The superior has an awesome responsibility. People go not by what he says, but by what he—

Acharati Practices

His behaviour sets the—

Pramanam	Standard, for
Lokah	the followers, the masses.

Shloka 3.25. Vidvan

Knowledge worker. Krishna recognises that the masses generally work, but with attachment. Managers often complain about how workers have become so materialistic and self centred that they play for overtime, medical reimbursements, etc. Before they can be changed, Managers, as knowledge workers, or even better, wisdom workers, need to provide an example of

Asakta chikirshuh dedicated work

Shloka 3.26. Sarva Karma

All work is important. The shreshtha must take care that he does not create.

Buddhi bhedam	Confusion in the mind and judgements of the less educated.

The Manager should avoid indulging in or encouraging loose talk about the company's top management, plans, policies, colleagues, partners, subordinates, etc.

Shloka 3.27. Ahankar

Egotism—Earlier, in 3.17 Krishna has emphasized the self and its importance. So, ego or identity as a psychological construct has its place. But not egotism. Managers are similar with the concept of a "prime mover," which activates other machines. Similarly, what drives human action?

Prakriteh gunih	The natural qualities of sloth, libido and refinement, in different subordinates.

But the Manager is in danger of imagining that "I" am doing it. His self is—

Ahankara vimood Clouded by egotism.

Recent organisational literature points out the danger of "them-ism," dividing the organization into "us" and "them." The *Gita* warns the Manager of the even more insidious danger of "me-ism."

Shloka 3.34. Raga and Dvesha

Attraction and repulsion. All our senses are attracted to some objects and repelled by others. The wise has to avoid or moderate both. The Manager is in danger of such love-hate duality with respect to dealers, suppliers, subordinates, seniors, peers, regulators, etc. He needs to find a balance, to be an objective and equitable decision-maker. He should take care.

Na vasham agached not to come under the speed of—

Ragadveshou likes and dislikes.

Shloka 3.35 Dharma Seema

Task boundaries. Here is one more *shloka* liable to simplistic misinterpretation.

Krishna emphasizes the desirability of

Svadharma	One's own allotted work; and the danger of taking on
Paradharma	Somebody else's work.

This has a number of potential advantages

- Specialisation, leading to higher skill and performance.

- Avoiding threat to each other.
- Clear career choices for new entrants.
- Partnership with others, with their own respective *dharmas*.

This is not against job rotation, career development and succession planning. All that is still within the *dharma* of business. But it is a caution against Managers dabbling in politics, speculation, religious or military affairs.

Shloka 3.36. Papam: A literal translation is "sin." The secular meaning for the Manager is "wrong action." Arjuna speaks for all of us, when he asks why man does wrong things—

Anichan api	Even though unwilling, at a conscious plane;
Balad iva niyojitah	as if pushed into it by force;
Kena prayukta	pushed by what?

Shloka 3.37. Kama and Krodha

Desire and anger. Krishna highlights two forces, in particular, which lead to wrong action—

Kama	Desire, endless desire. The Buddha also makes desirelessness the fulcrum of his entire teaching.
Krodha	Anger, spurring heinous acts.

Where do these two come from?

Rajo guna samudbhavah	Born out of rajas or feverish, demonic energy.

Rather than admiring and feeding these in oneself and

subordinates, the Manager should recognise these as—

Vairinam Enemies.

Managerial anger spills out in all directions. It creates stress for himself and other.

Shloka 3.38 Avrutham

Hidden. Some beautiful similes are given to illustrate how one's judgement can get clouded, such as—

Dhumena agnih Fire hidden by smoke.

Adarsho malena Mirror covered by dust.

Often, we find it useful to remind managers in training programmes of the need for

- Unlearning and
- Relearning, before
- New learning

Shloka 3.42 Shreni

The hierarchy. The *Gita* describes the ladder of existence.

- *Sthula shariram*—At the bottom is coarse body. One must keep it in good physical fitness.
- *Indriyani parani*—The senses are superior to the body. They need to be kept acute and refined, with the ability to appreciate the sense objects aesthetically.
- *Manah*—The Mind is above the senses. It needs to be trained to direct the senses towards the right objects, and to process well the sensory data.
- *Buddhi*—While the mind is subject to *chalana* (disturbance), the Intelligence is required to calm the *manas* and use its processing capability.

- *Sah*—The Soul is at the apex.

COUNCLUSION

The first three chapters of the *Gita*, dealing with Dilemmas, Knowledge and Action has lessons for managerial leadership. The key lessons may be summarised as follows:

1. The Managerial Leader should counsel his subordinates, when they are paralysed by hard choices.
2. Emphasise, observe and protect the Organisational *dharma* towards all Stakeholders.
3. Understand and follow *shreshtha dharma*—the Code of Conduct for the organisational elite. Set standards.
4. Practice balance in all extremes.
5. Always act without anxious attachment to personal benefits.
6. Cultivate qualities of *kausalam* (Excellence), *yogastah* (Concentration), *sthita prajna* (Steadfast).
7. Encourage *parasparam* (Interdependence).
8. Practice *samyama* (Self-Control).

Stand up, be bold, be strong. Take the whole responsibility on your own shoulders, and know that you are the creator of your own destiny. All the strength and succour you want is within yourselves. Therefore make your own future.

4

The Qualities of a Leader

Lessons from the *Mahabharata*

*S. K. Palhan**

This is based on a question as to why is Narada so much revered and respected which is asked by Yudhisthir in the *Mahabharata*, as was elaborated by Sw. Parmanada Bharati to a group of professionals and managers.

Narada is a grand strategist just as a leader also has to be. Generally in our films we portray him as a schemer and manipulator but it is not so. The fact is that Narada is an excellent strategist; which is a quality that all managers must have, to be able to manage things in an organization to meet specific aims and objectives. We should however note the

* Former Industrial Advisor, Govt. of India, presently, Director of Sri Sringeri Sharada Institute of Management.

difference between how a manager manages his work and how Narada does so. Narada is not serving any self-interest. He is doing everything for a higher purpose and never does anything for any selfish gain. Narada causes conflicts, only to direct the people involved towards the higher goal of self-realisation.

A good leader is also one who is prepared to strive and to extend himself for the sake of the spiritual development of himself or the people whom he manages. If you manage people so that both they and you grow spiritually, then this is the highest form of management. This is the ideal which we have to follow as leaders, as professionals and as managers.

Some of the other qualities we have to emulate to be an ideal manager are as follows.

QUALITIES OF NARADA

The more the knowledge and skill and goodness you have the more humility you must have. The less the ego, the more effective you are as a manager.

- Not indulging in sense pleasures but ever engaged in doing his duties.
- No trace of anger.
- Not resorting to restlessness and not undertaking unnecessary work, no extra movement of hands, legs, etc.
- Fearless.
- Not indulging in procrastination.
- Never be afraid or hesitate to do what is *dharma*.

- Fulfils his promises and forgoes his own gains or wants.
- Well versed in theory and practice required and acknowledged as an adept.
- Ever ready to forgive but not as weakness.
- Ever alert and energetic but not a slave to sensuous pleasures.
- Does not say unpleasant truth, Truthful, but because it is the truth he does not go on saying it, and speaks pleasantly and pleasing truth; does not lie merely to be pleasing and pleasant.
- Simplicity (but of nature that does not mean he is a fool or that he dresses in torn or outdated clothes).
- Is *susheel* (difficult to give an English equivalent but means full of good qualities.) (Prahlad promised to give and he was asked to give only his *susheelata* but when that was gifted, all other good qualities also left).
- If we practice any one *sadguna*, gradually all good qualities shall come. There is nobody who has no *sadguna*. At least one good quality is there in everyone, every animal, every plant, etc. By that one good quality that person can develop himself. Similarly, we must avoid even a single bad quality.
- Contented.
- Detached involvement.
- Moderate in sleep, food, etc.
- Speaks pleasantly.
- Does not have jealousy.
- Is sinless and does good to people.

- Does good without talking about it.
- Does not feel happy when others are in sorrow.
- *Samatvam*. Maintains his equilibrium.
- No strong likes and dislikes.
- He is full of joy and jokes but does not hurt anyone.
- Is a good communicator and explains things through verses from *Vedas*, to illustrate the points.
- Has forbearance. He forgives personal insults but not society or group insults.
- Takes action whenever a wrong is committed to anyone, not merely when it is against him.
- Does not insult anyone.
- Does not quarrel over money, woman, etc.
- Destroys all his faults.
- Has firm devotion to God.
- Does not criticise.
- Good communicator and orator.
- Never praises himself nor expects a reward for performing his duties. (Today in organisations everyone clamours for reward.)
- As a leader he is fully alert to see who is doing good/ bad work and is ever ready to reward and punish as needed.
- Soft spoken.
- Notices and observes strengths, faults of all but never tells faults of one to another. Does not speak unnecessarily of one to another.

- Has excellent judgement on what responsibility can be given to whom and to what extent without letting extraneous considerations like friendship affecting his judgement.
- Does not try to find faults in the *shastras* but has *shraddha* in its teachings.
- Has firm principles and lives without deviating from these.
- Never wastes time and thus sets a good role model for others to follow.
- Is always in full control of the situation.
- Has high standards and understands the essence of the *shastras*, and has a firm grasp of its application.
- Is always active, fully alert and is never careless or callous.
- Is ever conscious of the right time, *muhurta* and follows it exactly, very punctual.
- Is modest.
- Is ever interested in the well-being of others.
- Never reveals the secrets of one to another.
- Not a miser, does not indulge in self-pity.
- Is scholarly, without anger and without cheating or falsifying.
- Always happy either in loss or gain.
- Is unattached, with a firm mind and is expert and skilful in what he does.
- Is free from disease. Regular and moderate in habits—food, sleep, etc.

- Understands the value of time and makes full and good use of it.
- Knows the *atmatattva* the reality that he is the *Atman* and therefore a good human being.
- His world-view of reality is firm and based on the foundation of the *shastras* and therefore the whole superstructure of his personality is sound and perfect.
- Because his foundation and inner convictions are based on a perfect understanding of the truth therefore his whole life and personality are always directed towards the goal—the goal of self-realisation, which is the common goal of everyone. All his actions are based on *dharma* and he is ever striving to take everyone on the path of *dharma* to the goal—freedom. While *dharma* is different for different people and in different situations but because he is so well established in the foundation, his actions are naturally and spontaneously in accordance with *dharma*.

DHARMA

It is necessary today for managers to understand the complexities of *dharma*. Why? Because the managers are the leaders of the nation. It is their job to manage things. Specialists, professionals even administrators or politicians cannot be as good in managing things as the managers.

If managers are the leaders, and since it is their responsibility to manage then they have a lot to learn from the ideal managers—Rama, Krishna and Narada who is a master manager and whose qualities are being discussed. These qualities have to be our role model and these qualities are necessary in a good leader and an effective manager.

It is therefore important for the managers to get a flavour of Indian ethos in management. Indians have managed their affairs based on time-tested eternal values and qualities. Whenever these values are practised and applied India has been a leader in world affairs.

This is the challenge for the managers; to take India to its rightful position as the leader in trade, business and industrial fields once again, based on our own values which lead us to freedom. *We must give up the self-centred, money and greed oriented managerial systems of the West.*

LOVE FOR COUNTRY

At this moment of time the highest value is to learn to work and manage for the sake of building up our nation as a land of prosperity, once again. Love for the nation and the desire to work for its improvement is the one quality needed now. All other good qualities will be added unto you.

In whatever sphere you are working, always think how can you serve your country and its people. This attitude of service will uplift you. Do not think in terms of separate divisions, states, sects, religions, etc., we are all one. We love all humanity and this love we can express in our own workplace by doing our work for the love of our country, for serving its people and solving their problems. This alone will make us pure and give us peace and prosperity.

So long as the millions live in hunger and ignorance, I hold every man a traitor who, having been educated at their expense, pays not the least head to them.

5

Purpose of Life

*Sunil Kumar**

AIM AND PURPOSE OF LIFE

Let us try to understand, very briefly, the aim, purpose and goal of life so that we can evolve suitable managerial processes.

Unless we are clear on the goal how can we ever decide the path to be taken. Alice reaches a crossroad and asks Mad Hatter which road to take. That depends upon where you want to go, says the Mad Hatter. I don't know where I want to go, says Alice. Then it doesn't matter which road you take, says the Mad Hatter. This is our position. Alvin Toffler describes the Western society aptly–perpetual purposelessness.

* G.M., the PEC of India, Hon. Director, Vivekananda Centre for Holistic Management and Prof. and Course Director, Indian Ethos Programmes at Sri Sringeri Sharada Institute of Management.

Therefore we must understand the aim and purpose of life. Then only can we discuss the role of our daily work and dealings in achieving the goal.

OUR RELATIONSHIP WITH THE UNIVERSE

We have to understand first the three fundamental entities that is, *jivatma, jagat* and God and the relationship between the *jivatma* (the living beings, the knower, the subject), the *jagat* (That which changes, that is, the whole universe. The known, the objective world) and God. (The unknown).

To understand God we must note the major hurdle in understanding it:

- All of us, the *jivas,* are people with finite and limited knowledge and experience.
- Knowledge is infinite.

The problem is that the finite can never know the infinite. Only the infinite can know the infinite and the *rishis, Vedas,* scriptures only attempt to tell us. We amongst ourselves cannot know the infinite.

ONENESS AND INFINITE AS THE GOAL

We are told by the *Vedas* that God is infinite and though the *jagat* and *jivatma* appear different from God and separate are one and infinite. Infinite alone is bliss and as a *jivatma* I am here to try and realise my infinite nature in and through work and my life. This is the Goal. This is what all saints and all scriptures tell us. Of course we have doubts.

So let us hear about these ideas and try to understand these ideas or at least try and see the logic and rationale and think about it. This wanting to know and questioning attitude is needed.

FINITE CANNOT KNOW THE INFINITE

Firstly, let us note that all discussions between people with finite knowledge and experience based on incomplete and partial database is meaningless because the Finite will never be able to understand the Infinite. It is like six blind men holding six different parts of an elephant arguing amongst themselves what an elephant is like. They shall never be able to know what an elephant is like because of their partial vision.

However, a man who has eyes and can see the whole of the elephant can describe how an elephant looks like. But this description is also meaningless until and unless the blind men also see with their own eyes what an elephant looks like. Thus a person with holistic vision or a more holistic vision is needed to help our knowledge.

VEDA AS SOURCE OF INFINITE KNOWLEDGE

Is there then any holistic vision of infinite to guide us? Yes. The *Vedas* are the voice of the infinite and therefore the *Vedas* are themselves Infinite and not confined to any person or books. The *Vedas* mean knowledge; knowledge of the Infinite. They contain that Knowledge which cannot be known by the finite. All scriptures are attempts by saints and sages to explain the infinite for finite groups of people so that the finite people can understand the aim and purpose of life and be inspired to make themselves infinite. The proof of God is the statements of the *Vedas*. There can be no other proof because the finite just cannot know the infinite. That is why the great spiritual teachers like Krishna, Buddha, Christ, Mohammed all say that there is but one the God. Their claim that their respective message is the only word of the God is synthesised by understanding of the infinitude of the God.

SHRADDHA

What can we the finite people do. This is the question before us. We have either to reject all this and just carry on or we can have *shraddha* in our saints and sages and use our mind and intellect to listen to their ideas and try to understand them. If the logic appears rational and if we can believe that the saints and sages have love for us and want our good then we can even try and practice some of the self-development techniques. It is only when we ourselves experience, our doubts will go but to experience and test it, I have to put in some efforts.

FREEDOM TO CHOSE BUT BOUND BY CONSEQUENCES OF CHOICE

It is our decision. We have the freedom. We can chose to follow the selfish, immoral, lying, cheating, corrupt people or just the ordinary people or the selfish and self-centred scientists or politicians or rich leaders and industrialists of modern age. All these may be good people but with limited knowledge and experience. I can chose to follow the people or I can strike out on my own to face the world as I want to with my own values whatever they might be good, bad or wicked. The choice is entirely mine and as I think and do so shall I get the results.

With freedom of choice comes responsibility and accountability. This is the law which the *Vedas* and all scriptures tell us. Of course this also sounds as the only reasonable or logical way to explain different people and their status. It is our choice entirely and as I sow, so shall I reap-whether I believe in it or not. How can my happiness or sorrowness depend on anyone else? I alone am responsible for my pain and pleasure and I alone have to change to grow.

HOW SHOULD A WISE MAN PLAN HIS LIFE?

He should first and foremost after due analysis, fix the aim and purpose of life.

All his daily work and activities. All his dealings and interactions with people should then be such that it helps in reaching this goal. In Management the best path to the goal is termed as the critical path.

A wise man should therefore determine the critical path to the goal and then follow it.

An intelligent man recognises that as a finite person with limited knowledge he himself cannot determine the goal and the critical path to the goal. He, therefore, develops a longing and a yearning to know the goal and the critical path. He wants to know the goal and the way. People are of different attitudes and types and depending on their nature and their environment they adopt different methods. Of course knowing the goal and the way is one thing. Having the actual strength and determination to follow it is quite another. Therefore, *viveka,* the discrimination of knowing what is good and what is bad is needed and along with it the strength, courage and will power is needed to enable one to stick to the critical path.

For developing these qualities *sadhana* is to be practised, i.e., self-development. *Viveka,* practise and desire to succeed have to be cultivated through constant struggle and effort. Only heroes will succeed. But never mind failures. Arise, awake and stop not till the goal is reached.

OUR REAL NATURE

The saints and sages are people with infinite knowledge compared to common people with finite knowledge. They tell us that our real nature is one of infinite bliss, knowledge and existence. Today, we feel ourselves as limited and finite beings. We have forgotten our true nature of infinite joy and knowledge. But because we are infinite in reality therefore in and through all our activities what we are really seeking is happiness which is our real nature but *alas* we do not seem to be getting any permanent happiness from any thing finite. Those who have the holistic vision, the saints and the sages tell us that there is no happiness in any thing finite and changing. Infinite and eternal alone gives us real bliss. We have to recognise that each one of us has this infinite potential and unless we realise this infinite potential and manifest it in our daily life we will never be really happy or satisfied. If our true nature is of Infinite bliss how can we ever be satisfied with any thing finite. Therefore through our daily life we have to strive to overcome our finite nature and grow towards infinity. This is the aim and purpose of life.

WORK AS AN OPPORTUNITY

Our day-to-day work and dealings with people and problems is our opportunity for either growing towards infinite bliss or binding ourselves to the finite world of pain and sorrow.

The choice is ours. We may choose the short-term pleasant path of ordinary people or we may choose the long-term good path of the heroes. The road less travelled. The path of the *Rajarishis*, the saints and sages of whom we read and admire.

TQM VALUES

The Confederation of Indian Industry are spearheading the drive for excellence and improvements in quality and efficiency in Indian organisations. Their drive for Total Quality Management (TQM) is based on the Management strategies now being practised in USA, Japan, Europe, etc. They have clearly identified the following TQM attitudes and values necessary for excellence in action.

- Organisations exist in society for satisfying the needs of people in society.
- Profit is our compensation for satisfying the needs of society.
- Excellence, TQM, Team Spirit, prosperity cannot be brought about unless organisations and people practise the values of -
  - — Self control
  - — Respect for others, and
  - — Intellectual honesty.

We want to have successful professional lives so that we can maintain a high standard of living. In this era of globalisation and cut throat competition the values and attitudes needed for success identified above by hard core businessmen in USA, Japan and even in India are the same as are needed to keep us on the critical path to the goal.

"ONENESS" IN APPLICATION

If I want to be a good student, a good teacher, a good parent, a good professional, a rich and prosperous person the only way is to practice values and understand that profit is our compensation for service to society. What is society? *Samaaj*, which in Sanskrit means 'equal to God.' Why do I respect others? God is in me and God is in everyone of us. We are in reality one and not separate. If I deal with you, a customer, as partial being then you and I are separate but if I know that we are one in essence then how can I ever hurt you and not hurt myself. If I know that you and I are one then I will soon realise that any thing that I do to help others, to help society will help expand me towards my infinite nature and is a good action. Anything that I do for myself alone makes me a limited being and is therefore not in my real interest.

NOT BODY ALONE

We are in fact not the body, mind and intellect alone but we are the observer, and as observer, as witness we are all one with no differences whatsoever. When we attach ourselves to our body, mind and intellect we become separate. Therefore, the skill that we really need in life, which we may call life skills is to attach ourselves more and more to our true Infinite nature, as the changeless, eternal witness of the entire phenomena of change by withdrawing ourselves slowly, gradually from all the changes.

With this background let us now try to analyse the questions: Why values?

VALUES AT WORK

We have seen that the aim and purpose of life is to realise my infinite nature because that alone will satisfy me since that is my real nature.

Practise of values helps me to be on the critical path to the goal. The choice is mine and I shall reap as I sow.

In fact the scriptures tell us that *daana* charity alone gives prosperity. The *daana* may be in terms of money, time, knowledge, service to the needy and doing your work with the spirit of *seva* for the good of *samaaj*. *Daana* can be for the satisfaction of the body by *annadana*, etc., or for the mind, helping in education, or for spiritual upliftment, which is the highest. All these acts result in prosperity for yourself. You may earn wealth by hook or crook but you will never be able to retain or enjoy such wealth. Remember we are really wanting prosperity, not money and not wealth. Prosperity alone gives joy not money. Latest management techniques, TQM principles also clearly tell us that profit is our compensation for service to society and society, i. e., *samaaj* is equal to the God, as we have seen.

If you love and serve the country and the people you shall certainly be the recipient of prosperity. There is no doubt about it. In fact there is no other way for prosperity. Our problem is that we want to serve only ourselves or our family. If instead first we serve our country and our organisation, then our family and ourselves will be the beneficiary automatically. This is a universal law. This is *dharma,* i.e., the critical path to the goal.

Of course we don't all have to go out somewhere to love the country. If we practise values, if we strive for excellence, if we do our duty sincerely, if we are ever ready to help others surely we are showing our love and concern for our country.

The question is not of what the world is like but of what is my aim and purpose in life. In fact the world will always be a mixture of good and bad and like the dog's tail it can never be straightened. It is not the world but myself that I have to improve. The world gives me the opportunity to make my future. I can take the issue I face as problems or as opportunities for growth. I am free. I can face challenges, learn from my mistakes and example of others and make my choices and face their consequences. The world is a gymnasium to help my growth from finite into infinite at my own pace and doing my own thing. God has made man in his own image: says the Bible. I can be one of the herd or I can be the leader of the herd. The choice is mine and mine alone and I alone shall be ressponsible for my actions.

Again it is a question of "my" aim and purpose of life. The ideals are placed before us, for example king Harishchandra. Of course all of us cannot be idealist and we do fail very frequently. But God is very compassionate if we are really sincere. Failures do not matter. Only through constant attempts and the desire to improve we can change past habits and tendencies. What is needed is a firm resolve to do a thing. You may fail hundreds of times but the firmness of the resolve will help you to strive again and again; in the end you shall succeed.

Every moment of life we face a choice and depending upon the choices, we get the results. The fools choose short-term pleasure and the wise men prefer long-term good. The choice is ours. Of course, it is the motive behind our actions on which we get the results and not on the action itself. Therefore, if you are sincere and if you are having a genuine problem then the actions you perform under this critical conditions will be judged accordingly. However, if you can still withstand the pressure and maintain the right ideal then of course your reward will be the highest. Again the choice is ours. There is also a calculous for such reactions which says that for the sake of saving the family an individual can be sacrificed, for the sake of the village an individual family can be sacrificed and for the sake of the nation a village can be sacrificed, etc. The idea is that for the highest good the lower good can be sacrificed for meeting the critical situations.

Under the Indian scheme of education, the development of *viveka*, character and developing healthy world-view of reality and acquiring emotional stability through practise of self-development techniques is what is meant by education. This education must start from the age of six to eight when the child starts to develop the power of discrimination. It was at this stage that the child was initiated into the sacred *mantra* and through its repetition in a prayerful attitude sought the power of discrimination so that he could distinguish between the right and the wrong, select the right and develop the strength and capability of sticking to the critical path, to the goal. The right is the long-term good and the wrong is that which appears pleasant now but is not for our real good. The real is also the path of *dharma*. You will, therefore, see that it is only in the young age that the character is established.

Today our education is directed towards giving job skills only and there is no effort to give character education. The result is creating highly intelligent people but with no character. If you think, you will realise that you want people with character because it is only the good people who can really do good for every one.

In the situation that you are placed today what is to be done. You must find time, at least half-hour a day in the morning and evening, for contemplating, reflecting upon the values and ideals and practising some self-developmental techniques for your personal growth. At least this much you must do. To give an example in the *Mahabharata*, both Arjuna and Duryodhana are equally competent as far as intelligence and job skills and resources at their command. However, because the latter was fighting for his ownself he did not have a healthy worldview of reality and therefore he is considered to be a villain and did not win the battle. On the other hand Arjuna after teachings of the *Gita* was made to realise that he should put job skills for the use of society. He was therefore fighting for "others." He, who fights for "others" he who 'helps' others will always win and attain success and prosperity.

If I decide to be good and honest and have an intellectual conviction that this alone is in my real good then I will ultimately attract the good people. Of course, in initial stages it may not be so. But nevertheless I have to continue in my path though alone.

The ideal has been set for us by the holistic vision of the *rishis*. We are all people with partial knowledge and with plenty of weaknesses. Through practise, we have to reach the ideal. It may not be practical for us now but that does not mean that the ideal does not exist. The purpose of life is to realise the ideal and make it practical. That is the game that each one of us has to play.

The game of life has to be played by each one of us. In the ultimate analysis I shall be judged by how I played the game and not by how others play the game. The problems that we get in our lives are our opportunities to grow by facing the challenges as one does in the obstacle race. We may not be able to meet the challenges all the time and we can fail many times but we have to keep on struggling again and again and build up our strength. For this, *sadhana*, prayers, good character, etc. help.

In the *Mahabharata*, Yudhisthir represented *dharma*. He was always right and he was always good but he is not worshipped. The reason could be that his goodness was passive and was unable to produce results. We do not want passive goodness. What we want is aggressive goodness. The example of Krishna in *Mahabharata*, is the role model for us. Goodness must be played to achieve results. It must be used for developing strategies for results but through *dharma*. Therefore, you must fight the system. But fight not for yourself as mostly people are doing but for others which is good. This alone is the path which will give us peace and prosperity.

Let us analyse why people work. If you think for a minute you will realise that the activities you perform are only for the purpose of getting happiness. There is no other reason for doing work. Even when we are working to get rid of miseries we are actually doing so as to get happiness. If this is the purpose of work then should we not first analyse where happiness lies. Today, we think that happiness lies in objects outside. This is not correct. If you eat one sweet you like it and if you are made to eat hundred you shall not like it. How, could happiness then be in sweet. On the other hand you get happiness in your deep sleep.

Let us analyse the situation in deep sleep. Here we are not attached to our body, our mind or our intellect and therefore we can infer that real happiness can come only in such a situation. How to bring this detached state in our waking moments? This alone gives us happiness.

If the managers get the intellectual conviction and the power of *viveka* then only can they set up systems and organisational structures by which our organisations can become world class and compete with the MNC's who do not have the benefit of such lofty work values and ideals. If, instead, we keep on aping the west then we will remain second class and cannot become unique which is the quality needed to be the best. Therefore the need for Indian Management.

When you are doing any work, do not think of anything beyond. Do it as worship as the highest worship, and devote your whole life to it for the time being.

6

Ideals of Work

*R. S. Gupta**

History has shown and it is obvious from the deteriorating conditions all around us that spiritual ideals without material prosperity (conditions in India) and material prosperity without a spiritual basis (conditions in the world) both can do no lasting good to humanity. How to balance these two? This is the lesson we can learn from the philosophy underlying the work being undertaken by Ramakrishna Mission. It is these ideals of work which are needed by all of us particularly the enlightened managers and workers who are already engaged in serving.

Swami Vivekananda had a universal message for the whole world based on the eternal values arising out of the holistic vision of the sages which he has epitomised in the ideal.:

"Atmano mokshartham, jagad hitaye cha"

---

* Former Dy. Director General, National Productivity Council.

"We must strive for the freedom of the self and for the welfare of the world." This is the ideal to be followed in our work by everyone particularly the fortunate few who are already in the field of management. We in India have the responsibility to understand and practise this ideal and scatter broadcast these ideas.

THE BACKGROUND OF THOUGHT

If we can realise God by worshipping Him in images and symbols, it is all the more natural to realise Him in man through service to humanity.

God is all-pervasive. He is present in every human being. He is in everything in this universe and is yet beyond it also. Both meditation on the beyond and, worship of his presence in human beings can and, therefore, must lead us to God. This is the fundamental message of Vivekananda and the sages of all religions for all of us who work. The aim and purpose of human life "Be ye perfect as our Father in Heaven is Perfect" is the same for all humanity though stated in different ways. The art of *Karma Yoga* has been perfected in India and elaborates how we can achieve perfection in and through our work. The entire Indian Ethos is based on the ideal:

> "Through *Dharma* work to fulfil all your needs and desires and achieve *Moksha*, Freedom, Infinite Perfection."

On this background of thought we have to build our ideals of work.

If we work with this attitude of worship of God in and through our work then all our dealings with one another and all our work gets spiritualised. It converts our ordinary day-to-day work into a spiritual discipline which can take us to the highest perfection.

This vision should not be lost sight of in our day-to-day work, particularly in our service to humanity.

In the steel plant, the main objective is to produce steel. During this process various other by-products are also produced and give us profit; but these are not the aim and purpose of the steel plant.

PURPOSE OF WORK

Similarly, what should be the aim and purpose of all our work? Our aim should be to realise God by worshipping Him in man through service. This is the main objective of work. The welfare of the organisation, society even ourselves, though very important and necessary, is only a by product and should not be made the main objective. This is our ideal of work.

Our work should not even be mere service as an act of charity. Though this may be a good enough ideal this is not the main objective of our work.

Our main objective should be to realise God through work and this becomes possible when work is done as a worship to God. If we lose this spiritual vision our work will not be helpful to our growth. Of course, while working to realise God in and through our work we will automatically be doing some good to the organisation and the society but this is only a by product and is not the main aim and purpose of work.

We must not forget that the main purpose of our work, in whatever work we may be engaged in is to realise God and not merely to do good to ourselves or even to humanity through what is popularly called social service.

Serving the self, the organisation or social service is not the ultimate ideal, the ultimate ideal is the worship of God in man. If we lose this spiritual ideal then our work will degenerate into plain social work or worse into selfish work. We have seen that there are so many social work organisations, they spend millions and millions every year yet we know that no lasting good has come out of them. They have not been able to solve their problems because of the absence of spiritual ideal in their work. Working for self-interest or money is obviously no ideal, it is only a sign of weakness and ignorance and much as the West may like to project it as their motivation certainly this cannot be our ideal of work.

Therefore, spiritual ideal in our work should never be lost sight of. It is only this that converts ordinary work into a spiritual *sadhana*.

It is this spiritualisation which needs to be practised by all the leaders, the educated people, the professionals. These ideals need to be brought to the students and to the people. They have to hear of these ideals again and again, reflect upon it and meditate upon it.

We have to practise these ideals in our work places and create systems and an environment in our organisation where practice of such ideals are encouraged. We have to preach these ideals in our education systems, in our HRD programmes and everywhere. Unless individuals are inspired to practise these ideals at work the organisation and the society cannot grow.

This spiritualisation of work as an ideal will help everyone to keep his spiritual ideal intact and help him to work for his material requirements. It is our duty to practise these ideals and bring this message to people, our family, friends, colleagues, whosoever we may chance to meet.

AIM AND PURPOSE OF EDUCATION AND HRD

It is essential we have a clear concept of the goal of education. At present our education system has no goal before it.

What is given is mere academic knowledge. It's a job-oriented education, not value-oriented. It teaches only "Learning To Do" and ignores "Learning To Be." The fundamental purpose of education is to help man grow to perfection and this spiritual education finds no place in our education system. Little wonder then that our society is in such a chaotic situation. Everyone is complaining about indiscipline, corruption, greed, exploitation, violence, selfishness amongst students and adults. This is clearly the result of having no spiritual basis in our education and HRD systems.

In the name of secularism our children are denied all chances of knowing the ideals of Indian thought and work culture or practising self-development techniques for becoming perfect. We have to expose our children to the great cultural, moral and spiritual ideals of India and try to help them build their character. Prayers, meditations, reading the lives and teachings of saints and sages and getting established in regular *sadhana* for one's spiritual growth have to become a part of our education systems. Subjective spiritual qualities in students have to be encouraged and used for merit rating rather than mere academic scores.

CONFLICTS AT WORK

When we work together clashes are inevitable and do lead to discord also. Work then becomes a drudgery. Love for

God, Love for the ideal, commitment to realising the ideal and an intellectual conviction in the power of goodness, *shraddha,* have to be cultivated. If we love God then we do not mind these conflicts and continue our best efforts. Thus love for God, love for the self and family, love for the organisation, love for the nation, love for humanity is essential. To live peacefully amidst conflicts is great austerity and so we have to learn to adjust, adapt, accommodate and be balanced. Understanding the ideal of work will help us to retain our balance.

LOOKING FOR STRENGTHS

We must be generous about defects of others. We must focus on their strong points, the best side of the people we work with. That is always helpful in work.

The sagely advise is to look at others' faults through your heart (i.e., with love) and your own faults through your head (i.e., critically). Try to focus on the good in people and in situations and thus keep your mind pure. This practice is in itself a *sadhana* at work. It is based on the simple fact that God is the repository of all good qualities.

> "If you want peace, see nobody's faults. See your own faults. Learn to make the whole world your own." (Holy Mother).

How to practise this ideal at Work?

At work we meet all sorts of people. The point to remember is that the work should be done. It is not important that who does it. Many times we feel neglected that our claims have been overlooked. Many people tend to boss over us or take over our privileged work and we have to face many conflicting situations when we work. We must be on the alert to see we don't create conflicts or get into it with others.

We have always to remember that the work we do is for spiritual development, it is our service to God. Our work should not be to serve our petty ego or our self-interest alone.

Our real nature is one of infinite perfection and bliss and each of us have to manifest this perfection in our work. If we work to serve our petty ego then we create a blockage to the manifestation of bliss within us and this ultimately causes us sorrow.

In all our work, whenever we deal with others, we must be committed to seeing that our work is helpful to the spiritual development of others and ourselves. This is a complex task and requires tremendous self-discipline and dedication to achieve the highest perfection.

With this understanding of the aim and purpose of work our clashes in our work places can be gradually minimised. The organisation can run more smoothly when the people there understand and appreciate the ideals of work.

It is for every senior to hear of these ideals again and again, reflect over it and develop a commitment to working for this ideal in and through our work. This way our juniors will also be inspired and gradually the whole organisation will become prosperous.

To repeat, mere work, without the background of spiritual aspiration and meditation will bring only ruin and nothing else. It will only help to strengthen our ego and thus bind us more and more to this world. Let us be on the alert. Let us develop a discriminative mind to keep a check on how exactly we are working.

SELF INTROSPECTION

Before going to bed, review your whole day's work. Recollect what you have done, what you have neglected to do, how you have helped others, how much service in the real sense you have done, how much of your work was prompted by egoism, how much time you have given to God.

Try to spiritually analyse your whole day's work in this way and the next day try to remove the defects that were in your work the previous day. This is what Swami Brahmananda advises.

Of course, most of us do have such planning and review techniques for our professional work. The concepts of TQM (Total Quality Management), QC (Quality Control), Kaizen, etc., also teach us to practise, small improvements daily in our work. This is good but not good enough as an ideal. The ideal must be to spiritualise our work. Our work must lead to the manifestation of our infinite perfection. If we so work then profit will come, prosperity will come and our life will be really successful.

The more opposition there is the better. Does a river acquire velocity unless there is resistance? The newer and better a thing is the more opposition it will meet with at the onset. It is opposition which foretells success.

7

Understanding the Concept of Oneness

*Sunil Kumar**

It is a universal law that unless we know the total and correct picture, the holistic view, any judgement that we make based only on a part view can never be wholly correct and in fact is quite liable to be totally wrong based as it is on an incomplete and a part view.

It is therefore good to know the holistic view, the whole picture so that we may know the direction towards which we should work.

MYSELF AND OTHERS

These are the two basic entities we face in our life. It would be necessary therefore to know both these and their

---

* Compiled by Sunil Kumar.

relationship with each other, even if we exclude God, the unknown third element, from our reckoning. Ideally of course we must consider each of these three—*jeeva* (self), *jagat* (world) and God to get a holistic view for then alone can we correctly examine our long-term goals. Unless we do so how can we work in such a way that our work today is not only in the right direction but does not contradict the holistic view and in fact supports it. Ideally of course our managerial work and our dealings should be such that they become the critical path to the goal, and the short-term goals can therefore never be in contradiction to the long-term goals.

In this article we invite the managers to explore the highest flights of human intellect and get an intellectual conviction in the world-view of 'oneness' so that all our managerial processes can be reengineered to help us traverse the critical path to the goal.

ANUBANDHA CHATUSTAYA

A brief introduction to the subject, under (i) Topic, (ii) Utility (iii) Connection with you, (iv) Persons competent for it.

- *Topic of Discussion*
  - *Jagat, Jeeva, Brahman*

At first glance *Jagat, Jeeva, Brahman* look different from each other. *Brahman* is not known; it is a question mark. It will be shown that *though all are different and seem separate are in fact one*. It is *Paramatman* alone which is there. An intellectual conviction will be given that everything is *Brahman* alone.

- *(Prayojan) Utility*
  - Bliss.

- What do I gain by knowing the subject? If we analyse this universe, we find that no one is fully happy. Unhappiness is one word to describe the conditions of everyone. The gain is this: if we understand the *vishaya* we will get rid of all unhappiness and having got rid of it, we will come to our natural state, which is that of bliss. This is the goal of life. *Moksha*, characterised by a state of eternal bliss, there is no duality and therefore no possibility of unhappiness. Only eternal bliss.

Therefore the utility of the subject of discussion is that by understanding it we will get bliss which is *moksha*. *Moksha* is not something to be got after death. It is available now.

- *(Sambandha) Connection with you.*

It is addressed to all of us. Once we understand and know *Brahman*, (God) then we get *ananda* (bliss). There is *no other method* to attain *moksha*, other than understanding *Brahman*

- *(Adhikar, Yogyata) who is competent of understanding it?*

Will anyone who listens to the subject understand it? No. A special quality, preparation is needed. (This is so even in any professional knowledge.) What is the *adhikar* for this knowledge, this understanding? It is

Sadhana	*Chatustaya*	*Sampatti*	
Self effort to attain	Fourfold	Quality, possession	e.g. a wrestler's *sampatti* is his body, his physique.

WHAT ARE THE FOUR REQUISITE QUALITIES

• *Viveka,* • *Vairagya,* • *Samadishataka Sampatti,* • *Mumukshutvam.*

Viveka

Nitya	*Anitya*	*Vastu*	*Viveka*
that which always is — Eternal	that which is not always there —temporary	all that is. All objective entities.	to discriminate and to choose and act for the *nitya.*

To constantly examine the objective things and situations, to discriminate between them and distinguish between the permanent and the impermanent and with the help of *nischayatmika buddhi* to hold on to the eternal. Why? Because all sorrows arise only because we like to get attached to something which is by its very nature liable to change, and when it is no longer as we wanted it to be, we get *dukha*. We have to use *viveka* and attach ourselves to the permanent.

In all our worldly pursuits also we are always advised to have a long-term view, select something which is more lasting, than mere momentarily pleasure.

We therefore need to practise all the time by examining the *nitya* and *anitya*, even in relative terms and choose the long-term good over the immediate pleasurable. For example, if one is offered Rs. 3,000 as wages with no security or Rs. 2,500 with security, we are advised to choose the relatively more permanent, the latter.

The essential quality of choosing the permanent over the impermanent is a must if we wish to understand *Brahman*. To know *Vedanta* and to expound it well is of no avail if we do not have this necessary quality.

Vairagya

iha	*amurta*	*artha*	*phala*	*bhoga*	*viraga*
here	elsewhere in heaven	many things enjoy	fruit	enjoyment	no attachment to any of these.

to remain unattached, or to give up attachment to the (thought of) enjoyment of enjoyable things either here in this world or in the after (death) world.

Normally when we see an object of liking we become attached to it and crave for it. *Vairagya* means not craving. Even the desire to go to heaven after death has to be given up.

Samaadishataka Sampatti

(a) Sama

Control of mind; not letting it to be diverted to things here and there but fixing it only on the ideal.

(b) Dama

Control of external/sense-organs and fixing it on the ideal.

The quality of control over mind and sense-organs is essential for success even in worldly fields. Our attention is constantly being diverted through *shabda, sparsha, roopa, gandha, rasa*—these are the five sense-organs. These have been made outward looking, as it were, so that they constantly take the mind from the ideal. Even in studies, in business, we have to concentrate on it and not allow the mind to divert our attention in enjoyments.

Therefore if one is interested in *Brahman* then control of the senses both *jnanendiriyas* and *Karmendriyas* are essential.

(c) Upratti

Quality of enjoying only Brahman (*Upa*—resting only in God; *rati*—enjoyment)

Not attached to pleasures of the world (having seen their hollowness, impermanent nature), concentrating on bhajan, reading scriptures, talking of God, etc.

(d) Titiksha

Forbearance, capacity to accept things as they are. We are afflicted with *tap traya*—three types of distress; natural calamities; attack by others and death. Because of these three *dukhas* we develop *'dvesh'* : hatred / dislike for things and plan to get rid of it. But a man of *titiksha* develops the quality of forgiveness, acceptance, he excuses it. Of course he takes precautions and whatever action is necessary but is not unduly worried; when death comes also he bears it.

(e) Shraddha

Total faith in God, in the Vedas and in the guru who is imparting instructions about God with the help of the Vedas.

Unless I have faith I will not see God but I want to see God, only then I will have faith. This is a paradox. It is essential to have *shraddha* to know God. Therefore the advice is: have *shraddha* and then seek all answers, ask questions, satisfy yourself. But if you do not have *shraddha* and argue only for intellectual exercise than you cannot understand. Have *shraddha* in *Vedas* because it is the *Vedas* alone which can tell about *Brahman*, about God. There is no other way of knowing Him. It is because we are not able to reach this logical conclusion that we argue endlessly.

Therefore, the *shastras* advise to have total faith in the

Vedas and in the *guru* who is explaining it. *Shraddha* in *guru vakya, Veda vakya.*

(*f*) *Samadhana*

Poise, calm, peaceful.

Do not allow the mind to become agitated. It is a *sattvic* person who can maintain this poise. The *tamasic* person's calmness is due to inertia, stupor.

Mumukshutwa

Intense desire for *moksha,* total bliss. Generally we do not have this desire. We are familiar with happiness which is more like excitement and we only look for it.

Moksha or bliss is the state of balance and harmony, where there are no desires.

If one strives for *mumuksha* and has intense yearning, then all other qualities come to him, and spontaneously develop. This then is the basic quality required. To acquire it constant reflection is needed. *Viveka*; what is life? What is the meaning of it? This of course requires a very intelligent mind (not the intellect like knowing Maths, but wisdom). He questions what is the purpose of it, this round of birth, death, sorrow. Then arises in him the wisdom, intellect to desire *moksha,* and this is the sign of real intelligence; to be able to see through this universe of change, impermanence and sorrow and desire for the eternal, the blissful. It is a very noble, uplifting, sublime state; not a state from where one looks down, with contempt on others.

To learn *Vedanta* it is necessary to have proper guidance from a *guru,* because *Vedanta* is different from all other subjects, that we learn in this world. *Vedanta,* is concerned with our own selves. We have to experience ourselves. For this it is absolutely necessary that we consult someone, who has had a similar experience.

Qualities in a Guru: The *guru* must have understood *Vedanta* and must have experience. He must also have the capability of teaching it. He must be able to perceive the students' present state of knowledge, the doubts he has and he must be able to remove the doubts of the student(s). He must be a *shrotriya* (one who understands *shruti*), *Brahma nishtha* (mind always stays in God), *Sampradaya vit* (knows the tradition). It is very difficult to explain this experience and therefore it is important that it must be explained in a systematic method, which has been perfected over a long period of time. These systems have been thoroughly studied and perfected and its results have been fully tested. It is therefore important to follow a time tested tradition to understand this experience of that state which is changeless, eternal.

Gu means darkness *ru* means to remove, to bring light. Therefore the *guru* is one who removes the darkness of ignorance and brings in the light of knowledge.

METHODS OF KNOWING, *Pramana*

There are four different methods of knowing things *pramana* (Proof)

- The first is by the five sense organs: hear, touch, see, taste (*rasa*) and smell. This is the direct method known as *pratyaksh pramana.*
- The second is based on previous experience, inference and is known as *anumana pramana.* When we see smoke we know there is fire, otherwise there can be no smoke.

- The third is knowing things by example, *upman pramana.* for example, somebody who has seen a giraffe describes it to you. Then you go to the jungle or zoo and see an animal exactly as described. You are certain this is a giraffe.
- The last is ***arthapatti pramana.*** You are shown a man who is very fat and well built. You are also told that he does not eat. The two facts are contradictory and seeing the person you conclude that he must be eating. Thus when one meaning is told the other meaning should not be opposed to it and should not contradict. If it does, you conclude otherwise.

METHODS FOR KNOWING THE NATURE OF GOD

To know God none of the above methods apply, because we cannot see, touch or feel God. We cannot infer God by something related to it. We cannot give an example to indicate God just as we cannot give an example for sea or sky. The only method available is to believe the words of the Guru.

We find it very difficult to follow this idea, despite the fact that we learn things by someone telling it to us. For example, you ask the way to the market from a passer by, and reach the market by following the directions he has given you. This method of knowing does not feature in the four means mentioned above, *but it certainly works.*

Therefore the nature of God is to be known through the words of *guru*. This is the only method which is available to us. There is none other. Of course, we may question; how does the *guru* know? Well, he knows because his *guru* told him. Thus we go back in time. The enquiring mind who is sincere and logical as well as persistent in his efforts to know the truth will bring us to the start of creation and ask; how does the first man know? He has now brought us to the beginning of creation.

VEDAS ARE NOT OF HUMAN ORIGIN

How did the first man know about God is the question. The only logical answer is that he can know only if he is told by the Creator himself. This first telling by the Creator is the *Vedas* to the first person—Brahma. Brahma is a person of immense *tapas*, one of the greatest *rishis*, who has in the previous cycle realised the truth of the *Vedas* and reached this position of oneness with the Creator, who then entrusts him with the task of creation. The moment we make such a statement, doubting minds will say that we do not believe in all this. To understand that the *Vedas* are divine and not of human origin, there are five reasons, the logic of which is so strong, if you really understand it, that it shows beyond any doubt whatsoever the full logical necessity of this statement.

FIVE-FOLD PROOF

- No one has claimed the authorship for the *Vedas*. Every great name in the history of Indian Philosophy, has accepted the validity of the *Vedas*.
- Not only every word of the *Veda* is fixed, but every syllable and the rhyme for its chanting is fixed. To imagine that a body of verses can remain for ten thousand years without anybody ever thinking of changing it is unimaginable. We know from our experience that some tunes keep on changing and yet every *swara* of the *Veda* has remained fixed.
- This body of the *Vedas* is immense. It is so vast that we cannot imagine its vastness. If it is written into pages, it

will run into millions of pages. Further there are no contradictions in the *Veda*, which rules out the idea of different people writing it in different times. Even if we presume a single person has written it, then also there should have been contradictions because no man is consistent in his views.

- Therefore the very fact that there are no contradictions whatsoever in the *Vedas* is the fourth point which proves the fact the *Vedas* are *apaurusheya*, i.e., not touched by hands and therefore divine in origin.
- In addition there are certain statements made in the *Vedas*, which have been discovered by the scientific minds with the scientific equipment only now. There was no method of knowing these facts till recently and yet the *Vedas* have stated that it is so. The simplest example is the mention in the *Vedas* of seven islands of the world of which the seventh island Antarctica has been found by the modern world in 1911.

Therefore the *Vedas* are divine, and the only way of knowing God. These are statements by which we can know the nature of God. If the *guru* tells from the *Vedas*, then only we can respect him as *guru*. The *guru* must be *tattvadarshi*, someone who has realised the *tattva*, the truth and experienced it. He must be a knower of *sampradaya* and must be committed to maintain it because then only this subtle truth can be explained, understood and the tradition maintained in its purity so that it can lead the people to God through the optimum path.

Vedas contain two types of statement which are relevant to us, the first is *jnan vakya*. We have to understand the meaning of such *vakya* and, to understand it, we are free to question the *guru* till we understand these sentences containing wisdom, knowledge.

The second is the vidhi vakya. This is a direct instruction to us to do or not to do certain things. On these statements no questions and answers are entertained. For example, the *Vedas* say that to go to heaven, we have to do this. If you want to get this, do that and so on. For such statements we cannot argue and if we want this then if we follow the instructions, we shall get them. There cannot be answers to this question. But for our understanding of the *Vedanta* we have to use the *jnana vakyas*.

CAUSE OF THE UNIVERSE IS GOD

From what we know, only from that, we can know that which we do not know. Paramatma, the one God, can thus be known only through the Universe. Therefore the *shastras* give this relationship between the universe that we see and the *paramatma*. The cause of this universe says the *shastra* is *paramatma*. This is a fundamental definition.

Doubts: Some say that creation comes from *prakriti*, which is inert. How can an inert object produce itself? This is not possible as we know by experience.

The intelligence behind the universe: Whenever there is a motion there has to be *chetana, jnan,* intelligence behind it. For example, there is a book lying on the table, it does not move on its own. It is an inert object. To move it an outside force is applied. This force is also inert as for example when we move the book by hand, but beyond the hand is my intelligence. Therefore in our experience we see that whenever there is any movement, behind it, there is a force and beyond the force, there is intelligence. From this we can draw the conclusion that in this universe, behind this universe also there is intelligence. We can thus conclude that there is this intelligence behind this universe and we can accept the statement of the *shastras* that this intelligence is

God. But knowing this fact does not help us. Because it does not become our experience: we do not even know what is the nature of that intelligence. We cannot say anything about it till we ourselves experience it. Of course by *anuman* and by the *shastras* we are told about it. These are the only proof, till we ourselves experience it.

Universe itself is pointed out as this intelligence: In the *shastras* the question is raised; what is that, by knowing which all this is known? The questions are , how does it look, where is it? If you want to see it, the *shastras* say; here look! They point to the universe! We want to know the *paramatma* and we want to know the nature of *paramatma* and we are shown the universe, *jagat!* Therefore there is some relationship between the *jagat* and the *Paramatma, Brahman* and the *shastras* say that the *Brahman is the cause for the jagat*. Let us now try to understand this concept from the classic example of the pot, its maker and the materials from which it is made.

Understanding the Cause and Effect relationship (Brahman and Universe relationship) *Example of Creation of pot:* For creation of pot, there are three causes :

•	*Nimitta karan*	Efficient Cause	Pot-maker
•	*Upadan karan*	Material Cause	Clay from which the pot is made.
•	*Sahakari karan*	Instrumental Cause	Instruments used by the potter to make the pot.

These three are the causes for creation of all objects in this universe. When god wanted to create he became the creator, the pot-maker. So he is the creator of this universe and the efficient cause. We can understand it by *anuman pramana*.

However, by *anuman pramana* we cannot see that he is the material cause also, that is, the clay of the pot. In the upanishads the universe is said to be God, thereby stating that God is also the material cause. Thus God is both material and efficient cause. This is because *upadan karan is never different from the karya*. Pot is not seperate from the clay, knife is not different from the steel from which it is made. Gold necklace is not different from the gold from which it is made. Therefore the *effect is not different from the cause.* This same principal states that universe is not different from God, because God has made this universe out of Himself. "Let me become the many," as stated in the *upanishad.*

We should remember this statement which is the key to unravel the secret of *Vedanta—Karya karan se bhinn nahi hai. Karan karya se bhinn hai*— Effect is not different from the cause. Cause is totally different from the effect.

To understand this it means that whereas the pot is made of clay, this clay can be made into pot or any other item or it just remain as clay. The clay is therefore not the pot but the pot when broken into pieces or not is nothing but clay. Therefore if we are seeking God it is to be seen totally in the universe because the *shatras* say that God is the cause of the universe. But we should not make the mistake of thinking that God is the universe. Because God is the clay and the universe is like various pots, which may break and ultimately become clay. *Therefore God is separate from universe but the universe is not separate from God.*

Since the clay does not change its nature, but can be moulded into a pot, jar, plate, cup, etc., which can break and again become clay, the clay is the reality, the *tatva*, the *sathya.* Pot, cup are *Asathya,* because they change. *That which does not change is sathya.*

On the other hand, the pot is also a reality for our daily dealings. Therefore it is *vayavaharika sathya*. The problem is, we see the forms and forget the source. *Vedanta* tells us not to be distracted by the forms that we see in our day-to-day dealings, but to always remember that *tatva,* reality, is God.

The universe is not separate from God. When we see it so, it is our imagination, *avidya kalpit*. It is like treating a mirror image as real self, while one should always remember the real self. One must always distinguish between *sathya* and *asathya*. Between Brahman and jagat (Universe). Brahman is *nirguna,* no qualities, *sathya, nirakar* (formless) and timeless. *Jagat* on the other hand is *saguna* (with qualities), *asathya* (untruth, i.e., it changes), *agyan* (ignorance), *sakar* (with form), *jad* (inert) *anithya* (temporary). We see no qualities which are common between Brahman and *jagat*; despite being told that *jagat* is Brahman. There should be some commonality between cause and effect for us to understand that Brahman is the cause of this universe.

Let us see the example of sugar and *sherbat*. Sugar is solid, has shape, colour and a taste, sweetness. In *sherbat* we do not see the shape and colour of the sugar but we do taste the sweetness. Therefore we can say that the *upadan karan* of *sherbat* is sugar. Suppose the *sherbat* was salty, then there would be no quality of sugar in the *sherbat* and therefore there will be no relationship between cause and effect. *Thus for Brahman to be the cause of the universe, there must be one common attribute between the two by which we can recognise this.* Here comes another principle which we have to remember. If all the attributes of the cause come into the effect then can we say that an effect has been created? No, in that case, cause remains the cause. There is no change. For cause to be converted into effect, there has to be difference between them. On the other hand the difference should not be such that they totally contradict the cause. Because if they do there cannot be effect.

Therefore *whenever a cause is converted into effect, some qualities of the cause have to be lost but at least there has to be one common quality.*

To understand this common quality, let us take an everyday example. There is no similarity between a measuring scale and a roll of cloth. They are as different as Brahman and *jagat*. On the other hand when measuring takes place and a meter of cloth is marked from the total roll of the cloth, then the measuring scale and cloth become one, for we say we have *measured* one meter of cloth. Here the cause and effect are entirely different, and yet with one common attribute they have become one.

The common attribute between Brahman and the Universe is: existence; both are. So we are to admit they are one and the same. When we see a carpet and know it, we say that the carpet IS. It is totally different from Brahman, but it does not totally oppose it because *there is one element which is common to both, that is carpet is and god also IS*. This IS, existence, which is common to both makes the carpet, the effect, not different from God, the cause.

Maya is not an illusion as it is commonly talked of. It is a communicating link which makes us see the carpet as carpet and makes us think the carpet is separate from *Brahman*.

Maya is *anirvachaneeya*, i.e., from the side of the *Brahman*, it is *Brahman* and *Brahman* alone and there is nothing. But when you and I see it from our point of view, we see the carpet and the things of the universe and do not see the *Brahman*.

SPECIAL QUALITIES OF BRAHMAN

Even after all this analysis, we still see differences between God and the universe. We, therefore, need further analysis. Let us therefore examine the *lakshana* of *Brahman*. His special qualities. There are three special characteristics. The seeker now wants to know what are the specific qualities of *Brahman*. He is told that it *is satyam, jnanam, anantam. Lakshan* of something is more specific. *Lakshan* distinguishes it from everything else.

Shruti gives various contradictory attributes of *Brahman*. It says that he is smaller than the smallest and at the same breath that He is bigger than the biggest. It says that he is the shortest and in the same breath it says he is extremely tall and then also it says He has no size. It says that He is red in colour, then it says He is blue in colour and then it says it has no colour. It says that He is motionless and then again it says He runs.

The *shruti* is trying to tell us to look at *Brahman* directly. Do not look at it through attributes. For dealings in the world we know it only through its qualities, through something else and therefore it is that we have developed this habit of looking at everything, through its attributes. The *shruti* is trying to make us realise that there are no relationships, no qualities, no attributes; when we talk *of Brahman*. Suddenly we realise that what is being said is that *Brahman* is one and alone. There is no duality whatsoever. It appears differently to us because of qualities and attributes that we impose upon IT.

The message the *shruti* is trying to give is that no qualities belong to it. It is independent of all qualities and labels, free of all *upadhis*. The problem is that we can see it and look at it only by means of *upadhis*. Therefore by giving the different opposing and contradictory qualities we realise that it is attributeless, qualityless.

Another method of trying to understand this *Brahman* is the process of *neti neti*, it is not this, it is not this. Whatever quality you may ask of IT, the answer is it is not this, it is not this. Whatever exists of qualities, attributes, names or forms, characteristics is not it; then whoever is left is what *Brahman*, is. Out of *avidya*, ignorance, we think that the world is different. We know that the world is there. This is not to be negated. But you think it is different from you and therefore you think that you are seeing. This is *avidya*.

Let us remember once again, *karya karan se bhinna nahi*. But *karan karya se bhinna hai*. Effect is not different from cause, but cause is different from the effect.

To understand *Brahman* we have to see the clay as clay and not clay as pot. It is true that they are the same; but at this moment of time, we are trying to know the cause. In all the shapes and forms of a pot, clay is always present. But in clay there is no shape and form. The clay can be made into any shape and any form.

Now let us try to understand the *lakshana* of Brahman, in our awaking, dream and deep sleep states. In the deep sleep state, I do not know anything. I have no attributes, qualities, shapes and names at that time. This is the nearest way to the state of *jnana*. In the awaking and dream states knowledge is because of *visheshana*, there are different objects but in deep sleep there are no *visheshans*, it is *visheshan rahit*. We are not conscious then and only on awakening can we explain the experience of the dream and sleep states. The experience of *jnan* is one and the same. This *jnan* is not intelligence. Intelligence comes only with *visheshan* but the *jnan* we are talking of is without qualities. When this pure *jnan* combines with *buddhi*, it is *viseshan*, *buddhi* without *viseshan* is equal to *jnan*, is equal of *satya*, is equal to *ananta*.

Swaroop of *Brahman* is *nirguna*, it is *neti, neti*; in it all the *upadhis* are removed. You understand it by *sadhana*, by *Sharanagati*, by child like simplicity, and *shraddha* in God.

Therefore the only way of knowing it is *anubhav*. You try it, experience it and, then you will know it. When I ask a person, who he is, he will give his bio-data. But when we are dreaming then who are we. When we go into deep sleep what we are; you cannot describe it. Similarly *Brahman* is also undescribable. We can of course experience through *shravana, manana*. Perhaps you can say that by *sadhana*, by *sharanagati*, by *saralata*, simplicity, by *shraddha* in God we can experience *Brahman*.

We try to look for Brahman everywhere excepting in our own self. We forget we ourselves are Brahman. We have to realise *Aham Brahmasmee, I am all this*. This is the reality. It has to be reflected upon, understood and imbibed in ourselves.

Just as we say my child, my father and my mother, in the same way, the truth of the matter is *aham brahmasmi*. Let us try to understand this. During waking and dreaming everyone of us is different and we have different experience. However in deep sleep we have all the same experience at all times. This experience of deep sleep is same for everyone. It is free of space and time. This experience of deep sleep has nothing that changes. This is one of the *lakshana* of *Brahman*, i.e. It does not change at all any time, It is the same. Now we find that this changelessness is a quality and an attribute. An experience which we face everyday whenever we are in deep sleep. Therefore I have in me one of the *lakshana* of *Brahman*. Remember we had seen that effect must have at least one quality of the cause and *Brahman* is the cause with changelessness as an attribute which we also have.

The other *lakshana* of *Brahman* is *jnan*. In the waking state *jnan* is of *visheshan* in the deep sleep state jnan is *nirvisesh jnan*. If I ask you for your experience in deep sleep, you will say that I do not know anything. This *jnan* that 'you do not know anything' is also a *jnan* and this is an attribute of *Brahman*.

In deep sleep there is also *ananda* because when describing deep sleep you can say nothing of your experience but that you have enjoyed your sleep. During the deep state all attributes have left you. You have become smaller than the smallest, bigger than the biggest and all contradictions can be reconciled in the state of deep sleep just as the contradictions are reconciled in *Brahman* also. Thus we see that all the *lakshana* of *Brahman* are there in me also. Therefore I am *Brahman, aham brahmasmi*. Having explained through all these different methods that I and *Brahman* are the same, yet I am not able to experience it. This is *avidya*. The only way to understand this is to keep on trying again and again. Realise that we can see only the *saguna roop* not the *nirguna roop*. Our duty is to keep on struggling to know Him. It is difficult no doubt, but then there is no other way. God is the *karmaphaladata*. *Jnan* also is his *kripa*.

Simplicity, straightforwardness, simple, sincerity, humble to the core and no tension whatsoever are required.

The *ajnan* that we have is not knowing the *swaroop* of *Brahman*. From the beginning of period of time we have had this ignorance. But this ignorance has an end because as we have seen that we have to realise our identity with *Brahman*.

Brahman is not a worldly person. Therefore I also cannot

be worldly. If I and *Brahman* are said to be the same then does it mean that *Brahman* is a worldly person like me. We are told that it is not. The only truth is that I am also not worldly but *Brahman*. The conclusion to be remembered at all times is the following :

Jeeva (-) *agyan* = *Brahman*, God, *Paramatma*

Again and again we have to tell ourselves that you are not the body, you are different from the body; never identify yourself with the body, mind and intellect. Remember that you are *Brahman* and therefore your nature is infinite knowledge, existence and bliss. If somebody insults you, again remember *I am not the body, I am the Brahman whereas he is insulting the body only*. In this way we have to keep on identifying ourselves with the *Brahman* at all times and keep on remembering that all the qualities imposed upon me are in relation with the body. Various spiritual practices helps; *selfless work, mantra japa,* for example will lead to *chitta shudhi.* We have to be constantly up and doing. *Svadhyaya, shravana, manana, nidi-dhyasana* has to be done continuously.

We must understand that *maya,* is not *avidya. Maya* is there as a power of *Brahman. Avidya* is mine and is to be removed. *Maya* is Devi. It is there and It has to be crossed by her Grace. Many people feel that to be a *sakshi,* to be a witness is the end, the goal. It is not so. What we have to realise is *aham brahmasmi.* Being merely a witness without knowing *Brahman* is not enough. It is through the mind that we see, but mind is not the end. We always say my mind was not there. Therefore, it is a possession of mine. It is not myself. It is an Instrument that is being used by me and therefore mind and myself are two different things. We can also see that when we are asked to still the mind we fail to do so. But when we are in deep sleep after crossing the dream sleep our mind becomes totally still. Therefore merely stilling the mind is not the goal. The *atma* is beyond the mind. *Sakshibhava* is not *moksha*. Experience of *Brahman* alone is *moksha*. The mind and *prana* are in close proximity and therefore if you could control the *prana* then the mind gets control. But this is far from enough in the experience of *aham brahmasmi*. The problem is that the *vishvas* comes when mind understands. But the mind is limited and therefore fails to understand *Brahman* which is *nirakara,* and infinite. Mind has to itself become infinite.

Shravana and *manana* is what is required. No *yoga* is really necessary. To know and understand *aham brahmasmi,* no intellect is required. No book knowledge is required. And there are no short-cuts; *shraddha,* sincerity is all that is necessary.

Our problem is that we are never able to put in the effort. We do not struggle to know it. We allow doubts to come in. We do not accept the statements made by the *guru* and the *shastra,* and our mind keeps on bringing doubts and questions even after we have understood the nature of *Brahman* and intellectually accepted it. We have to be intellectually convinced that it is correct. Once we have done so we have to bring some sense of discipline in our life. We have to follow some simple rules, have humility and keep on trying to understand it. Do some *pooja* or *mantrajapam*. We have to find time for it.

What I want is muscles of iron and nerves of steel, inside which dwells a mind of the same materials as that of which the thunderbolt is made.

8

Self-Development

*Sunil Kumar**

Self-development is a popular term today in Management and Human Resource Development. However no one in the Management or HRD fields is clear on:

(i) What is 'self' and what is 'development' and therefore there is no clarity on,

(ii) What is the direction towards which 'development' should take place to signify progress and development of the self.

Therefore even though Management experts today talk of self-development there can be no development until and unless we are clear about the 'self' and about what exactly is meant by 'development.'

Today in the modern age the fact is that we do not have any clear concepts of the 'self' or the direction of

* GM, The PEC of India Ltd.

'development' and we have wrongly started believing that dams, power stations, large automobiles, factories, etc., are signs of development and growth! In pursuit of such ideas of growth we have spent all our energies since Independence. Have we reached anywhere? Have we solved any of the problems of society or have we created more and more problems? Have we produced nobler people in spite of all our education and technology or have we ended up by destroying all that was good in the people?

Today, in the pursuit of modern factories and consumer goods we have given up our duties and keep on clamouring for rights. We have no *shraddha* in God, we do not believe in rebirth, we do not believe in the universal and eternal human values or the oneness of universe which are integral parts of Indian culture. The systems of marketing and advertising create more and more desires and they build up a false set of needs. The social systems do not lead to austerity and simplicity; only they make us more greedy.

We are always seeking only physical comforts, and getting more comforts is being considered a sign of development. We have forgotten the worldwide principle of "simple living and high thinking." Our leaders love to spend money for their comforts but have nothing to give to the people except their own bad characters.

We have created divisions amongst people—rich *versus* poor, owners *versus* employees, managers *versus* workers and unions, etc. Can all these conflicts be termed development?

The communist regimes believe that the workers alone can work for the good of the people and so they must unite and fight the rich. They believed that the state will wither away when workers unite and we see in former USSR and China that the state has become even more powerful and the workers continue to be exploited. In any case the communist experiment has already failed. But this does not mean that the capitalist experiment of the West is any better. For example, the USA have achieved tremendous production, excellent technology, roads, cars, films, supermarkets, computers, etc. But already we know that the society is falling apart because of violence, sex, drugs. American family life has broken down. Poverty is growing and many poor people are prepared to work only if they can get food to eat. Unemployment is increasing and most of the Americans are not even going for higher studies and 50 per cent of college seats are being taken by foreigners.

Therefore, the Western systems and experiences that have failed within the last few decades cannot be said to be time tested. Americans have had to suffer no exploitation, no wars, no epidemics and yet why have they gone into billions of dollars of deficits? Why do Americans have to start wars to maintain their prosperity and their industry? Why is unemployment and poverty increasing by leaps and bounds?

We therefore must clearly understand that there is something basically and fundamentally wrong in all the present and modern systems—our education systems, our management and HRD systems, our concept of self-development—all these need rethinking.

THE FOUNDATION

In the modern age the relation between self and the society; self and others; Me and works; And who am I are not clear and not defined.

Unless we first understand and settle these basic and fundamental questions the foundation of our personality can never be sound. Unless the foundation is sound the superstructure can never be sound.

On the one hand it would appear that the top of the superstructure is far away from the foundation but it should not be foregotten that it is also totally dependent on the foundation.

In Indian Ethos "Who am I?" is the foundation. Therefore the first task is to build it up. Only then can we be in a position to define self and deal with others. This questioning and understanding of "who am I?" is a spiritual question and we cannot avoid becoming spiritual if we want to build up the foundation of our personality.

Do we have a goal? To start with we should note *vasudhaiva kutumba*—that there must be a common element within each of us and there must be a universal and common aim and purpose for everyone of us because only then can we discuss this question of self-development 'together.' Here the Indian ethos has a lot to contribute because it asserts the unity of existence, an interconnectedness of everything. It clearly identifies the common goal and the critical path to it. "Through *dharma* enjoy *artha* and *kama* and reach *mukti*, the goal of all." If we are all different and have different aim and purpose then we cannot sit together and discuss the process of self-development. The Western ethos does not have this common and universal goal in view and therefore in their cultures division, separateness, mechanistic concepts dominate all work and life.

This fundamental goal of all of us cannot be put to vote or left to be decided by discussions because the fundamental and common fact is that we do not know who we are, from where we have come, where are we going, why we are here, what is our relationship with others, with nature, etc. How then can we decide this fundamental issue?

For this we have to become spiritual. There is no other way because all of us have only a partial knowledge and we know that partial knowledge cannot ever reveal the total, holistic picture. And unless we decide this question, we cannot build up a good foundation, a true picture of the reality and we need a good, clear-cut "world view of reality" to be able to direct our efforts for self-development in the right direction. We have therefore to depend on people with a "holistic knowledge" to guide us and this needs *shraddha,* respect for the words of the illumined masters.

LET US NOW EXAMINE OURSELVES

Is my dress myself? No. Am I the body? If so I must pamper my body. Then development would mean a good body. But body keeps on decaying and however may I develop it, it will decay and die. If I am the body, then self development does not really mean much. The same applies to all my organs. The spiritual reality is that I am not the body.

I am not the Body

From this it clearly follows that development has nothing really to do with body. How can comforts, pampering to the body then be called development? And if we only think a little, we will soon realise that all present systems are really caring for the body and in our ignorance we take it to mean development. We now see that this is not so.

If I am not the body then am I the *'manas'* (that part of the mind which only inputs the sensory data)? No; if I am the *manas* then development would mean acquiring more and more information, like a computer. Can it be myself?

No. Then what about myself being *buddhi* (that part of the mind which discriminates and decides) or *chitta* (the part of the mind which stores all the data received). We are not these either. Many times I do not remember nor do I understand. Therefore I can appreciate that I am not the body and not the mind.

Let us continue with our examination to know *Myself* who am I.

When I go to sleep I lose contact with the body. As long as I retain contact with the mind, I dream. But in deep sleep I stop all my contacts with the body and mind.

In deep sleep I am all alone with my true self and have no connection with the body or mind. In this state I am all alone. When I am all alone I enjoy the most. I cannot explain about this state for, even the mind, my instrument of perception is not there and so I do not still know who am I. Nevertheless I know that deep sleep is very refreshing and relaxing. I am not able to do without deep sleep. But I realise that though I enjoy being all alone in deep sleep I am totally ignorant of myself, *ajnan, avidya* are my problems. Unless I can solve this problem I cannot decide on my self-development.

Here again the Indian ethos categorically asserts that my true nature is infinite knowledge, infinite bliss, and infinite existence. The infinite bliss, happiness, that I seek outside is my own real nature. Of course we do not realize it and this is our problem—Understanding that happiness is in our own self. Everyone of us is pursuing happiness and all our activities are directed towards this end. This is the common and universal goal for all of us. We are pursuing happiness because that is our real nature and we will not be happy until we reach it. It is therefore necessary to understand the nature and source of happiness because it seems an integral part of "self" from logic as well as it is asserted to be so.

Normally we perceive that happiness lies in things and objects and we look for it in this world. But a little analysis will show that happiness does not lie in things outside but is within us. We become happy or unhappy in the presence or absence of objects. The question is did the thing bring me happiness, or was happiness already within me which just surfaced at that occasion. For example, one sweet will bring me happiness but if I eat ten of those sweets my happiness certainly will not multiply tenfold. In fact I would rather start feeling sick. Hence, this shows that there is no direct co-relation between sweets and happiness. There is happiness already present in me which surfaced due to sweets at one time or some other object at some other time. Further it is interesting to note that the sweet does not create any sensation of happiness in the sweet-box, the table, plate or the spoon, only in me, as happiness is already present in me.

If happiness is within us then 'self-development' would mean "maximizing this happiness within us." Let us see when is this happiness at its maximum. It has been considered and numerous experiments have proved that sleep is one thing we cannot do without. We need our daily sleep. It refreshes, relaxes and makes us fresh. We may eat all kinds of delicacies, acquire all types of things to enjoy, but if sleep is denied to you, you will be willing to give up everything for a good night's sleep.

In deep sleep, we are all alone. We have nothing at all with us. Not even dreams. In fact when we do not have deep sleep we say we had a restless night's sleep but the moment we go into deep sleep, we are all alone and because we cannot do without it, we must be the most happy person at that time of deep sleep. People who have been denied sleep have realised that sleep is the most important thing for us. Since we do everything for happiness it follows that our desire and dependence on deep sleep is only because it gives us maximum happiness, though it does not seem so unless we think about it a little. Thus we can see that—happiness is within us and that the happiness we get when we are all alone with no attachment to anything is the maximum.

Development is linked to Happiness

Based on this fact that happiness is within us, that it is maximum when we are alone and unattached, the definition and the direction of development can be given. Development would then mean to get rid of everything because, as we have seen that gives us the maximum happiness.

This is the hard reality. When in deep sleep we are all alone, unattached to our body and mind complex. Then we forget all our pains, miseries, problems and we are totally at peace with ourself and happy. This is the state which we crave for most. We somehow miss this obvious conclusion and start searching for happiness in outside things.

It is this knowledge of the source and means of happiness which is the foundation of Indian culture. That is why *tyaga* is emphasised and a *sannyasi* is given the highest respect, love and reverence. The king is the person who has all the things, power and the glory and yet Indians idolise not the king but the poor *sannyasi* who owns nothing.

The great Alexander came to India, was drawn so much to a *sannyasi* that he offered him vast riches, power and glory but the *sannyasi* refused everything. The *sannyasi* was established in the truth that true happiness lies not in any object outside but is within ourself, and we can enjoy this infinite happiness within us only when we are not attached to anything else outside.

The truth is that simple living and high thinking is the ideal everywhere. Everyone admires a person who is not attached to things.

It is only in the recent times that the American led culture tells us that "possess and you will be happy." Marketing, advertisement, mass scale production, produce and throw away, ever changing fashion, exploitation of nature and waste—and all this only to suit our greed and wants—are all the result of this wrong philosophy which seems to think that body comforts will bring us happiness!

The Indian ideal is a *yogi*, free and full of infinite bliss and happiness. The modern Western cultures have ignored this simple truth. It has made our lives so complex and full of unnecessary needs that the result is stress and strain. People are not happy and therefore they have not developed themselves even though they may have developed many things.

To get happiness, do we then sleep?

People generally blame the Indians of being inactive and on their religion which says that happiness is maximum when you are asleep!

Of course we do not say we should sleep to be happy! But nevertheless this example of sleep gives us a glimpse of that blissful state. We have to learn from this experience that happiness is maximum when we are detached and are in our own true nature. This is an experience we have to bring to bear in our life. In the midst of all our problems and actions we have to remember that to be happy, we should be unattached to our surrounding and emotions. By constantly thinking like this we will learn to be happy always. This can be explained as a kind of detached involvement. For example, when a mosquito bites us, we spontaneously remove it. When we decide to go to office, we are thereafter acting spontaneously and our whole mind goes into automatic gear. We are involved in the beginning and during the journey we have a detached involvement. If there is any obstruction or hindrance we take corrective action but otherwise during the journey we act with detached involvement. For example we are not thinking all the time of having to turn left, or right and so on.

This decision a "*sankalpa*" taken at start of an activity sets the goal, plan of action, strategy to fulfil it and what will be the fruit of the action. All these are considered and a "*sankalpa*" (firm resolve) for action is taken. Thereafter we concentrate on the action and do not keep on thinking "I want this result." Thus after *sankalpa*, decision and strategy for action we act spontaneously with a detached involvement. We delegate different duties to people at work. After the initial *sankalpa* our role is to be a witness, with not much interference. This role of being a witness, free from body and mind is to be practised.

We have to learn to be a witness, to withdraw from the body, mind complex and identity ourself with our real nature, that which gives, happiness in deep sleep. We have to identify with that happiness in the midst of our actions and problems because that is our real, true nature.

Once we know that happiness is our real nature we have to practice identifying with it. Our problem is that we wrongly think that we are the body, mind complex. Therefore I am not able to withdraw from it. We have been identifying ourselves with the body, mind complex for such a long time. Now we have to detach ourself from the body mind complex and tell ourself 'I am not the body mind complex, I am the infinite bliss.'

Development for Happiness

Self-development really means becoming aware that our real nature is of infinite happiness and we have to detach more and more from our body mind complex and attach ourself to more of our real nature which is of infinite happiness. This is the foundation for development and the foundation of the happiness that we seek.

I am the self. Only when we remain in our nature, detached and alone do we experience ourself which is of the nature of infinite happiness.

When we are attached to the infinite self then for us, no action is needed. But when we are not fully aware of this then we have to act.

The purpose of all our actions is therefore: to become aware of our identity with our real nature. Which is one of infinite bliss. This is the goal, the ideal we have to reach.

Who am I and the Aim and Purpose of Development

This knowledge now enables us to understand our self and its development. Ourself is not the body mind complex but it is of the nature of infinite bliss. Self-development therefore means to realise ourselves as infinite bliss.

Therefore the purpose of self-development is to realise ourself as infinite bliss

All our actions, all our work, all our duties must therefore be such that it helps us to realise ourself as infinite bliss and detach ourself from thinking that we are the body mind complex.

Once this awareness comes then we have to fix once and for all the aim and purpose of our work and life which is to realise our true nature as one with infinite bliss, joy and happiness.

The path: How to realise our true nature? *Dharma,* is the path laid down by the people, who have realised. If our actions are in conformity to the *dharma* laid down for us, then this is the critical path to the goal, the path of *dharma. Dharma* stipulates the critical path to the goal by giving details of how we should and should not act. Indian Ethos alone helps us to understand the goal of life and fix our direction of development.

The modern age and Western cultures do not have this clarity of thought and are fooling the people by their glittering objects. We should not fall into this ignorant trap and be led away to our destruction. The Western cultures are looking for the black cat in the dark room which does not exist. No happiness can be there in any of the material goods that the West so proudly considers as the signs of their development.

The Western cultures do not know the meaning of self or direction of its development. Let us not follow their foolish example but let us be clear on the self and direction of its development based on the universal and eternal values and principles given to us by our great *rishis*.

Take sex. It gives us great happiness. So the West says enjoy it and they teach young children in schools now to have safe sex! *Dharma* says, no sex while you are studying. Enjoy it to the full only as a householder. But do not indulge in it as a *brahmachari*. Why are they saying so? Because they are clear on the meaning and direction of self-development. Self-control alone leads to happiness. Children must learn self-control, students should not indulge in sex. People who have no idea of the aim and purpose of life are out to misguide us and we get carried away.

Yama, niyama, self-control, *ashrama dharma, purushartha* are very well thought out systems to guide us gently towards realising our infinite nature. The Western cultures have no clear idea of the direction of growth *therefore we cannot follow their self-destruction methods which to them is self-development.*

THE INDIAN CONCEPT OF SELF DEVELOPMENT

We must note that Indian civilization is tens of thousands of year old. It has survived so long only because it is based on eternal values *sanatana dharma*. The whole society has got a clear cut direction and a common purpose.

Through dharma, enjoy wealth and fulfil your desires and realise that your true nature is infinite bliss. This is the goal and the path laid down.

Everyone has his *dharma,* duties, to perform and code of conduct both at home and at work.

The *shastras,* specially the great epic, like the *Mahabharata* and the *Ramayana* give the *dharma* for all types of people and this *dharma* is not based on the partial knowledge of people with partial knowledge. It is based on the directions and guidelines given by people with holistic knowledge, the infinite knowledge.

The Indian ethos prescribes *dharma* even for robbers. It says do not kill women and children, do not kill people who surrender, give 25 per cent of the loot for the common good of society, 25 per cent for temple, etc. Every robber who strictly follows the code of conduct as stated by the *shastras* shall be purified.

Thus *sanatana dharma* controls every fabric of Indian society. That is why though the majority of the Indian population is poor, the percentile ratio of their committing crimes are much lower than that of so-called developed countries. The soldiers of India also do not resort to violence, exploitation, etc., as these are not a part of our culture. They also have a code of conduct as the *Mahabharata* brings out. Now of course no one follows the *dharma*. For this the blame is on the leaders of the society who have themselves stopped following *dharma*. The simple villagers, the vast strength of villagers of India are still good people and the moment the leaders of our society stop following the greed and exploitation of the Western cultures and start following the age-old universal *dharma*, the country will again become the best because we still retain all the best values and ideals based on the holistic vision of the *rishis*. This *dharma* must be learnt and followed by us, the educated people.

We have to be clear of what is self and what is development. Happiness is the Goal of all. We need not run after things because happiness is within ourselves. To manifest this infinite happiness in our life we have to respect the goal and be guided by the *dharma* laid down for us. Through all our work and mutual interactions, all our enjoyments, all our desires, all our wealth we must apply principles of *dharma* and keep our aim as freedom, realisation of infinite bliss.

Indian ethos is grand and glorious because it fixes the aim and purpose of our life and guides us on the critical path to the goal.

People say that India is poor. But it was earlier a leading nation. Even Columbus was searching for India—why? Not because we were poor but because we were very rich.

- What is the message for us, the professionals and the managers?

Let us use all the modern techniques and tools but let us always remember the direction of our goal. Of course a person who realises his infinite nature, need not be an expert manager. Self-realisation is the goal of life and fixing this goal helps us to conquer all our bad qualities. So that our judgement is not adversely affected by our likes, our anger, etc., and our discussions will always be fair, impartial, just and good.

Today we believe very much in democracy which is not at all a good system. The evils of democracy are obvious in our societies whether in USA or a poor country. Democracy has to cater to the weakness of people. Only the monied people, the corrupt can get elected. Slogans, publicity, etc., are used to hoodwink the people. People are degenerating. No one of calibre, no noble people are now left in the democracies. USA has stopped producing great people.

Take population and education: The fact is that when standards go down, then population increases. The world over population is increasing and this shows that the world civilisation is not progressing but becoming worse. Lack of good, character building education is also a cause of increase in population.

Take family planning. All the birth control measures lead only to debauchery, over indulgence and they allow people to enjoy without any sense of responsibility or self-control.

All these systems of the West are not of self development but for self-destruction.

It is the top management which is the foundation of organisations. They have to lead the way, bring simplicity in their lifestyle. Simplicity leads to detachment which results in achievement. The highest level of people are those who are selfless. They are devoted to work for the good of others. They do not identify themselves with their body mind complex but realise that they are one with the infinite. The more unselfish a person the greater is he as an achiever and his work lasts longer. Take the work of Rama, Krishna, Buddha, Christ. Take the work of great industrialists of our country. They were also more unselfish and selfless than the common run of people.

Self-development must start from Childhood

The first five years of a child must be used for character development, prayers, strotams, *bhajans*, stories, inspiring, character building stories from the *shastras*. Children are pure, they learn by observation and therefore as parents we have to set an example. Competition is not good and cannot be healthy and Indian ethos talks of cooperation and sharing, not competition.

For example in a village, the elders, even today, do not use a razor as they would then prevent barbers from their livelihood. A barber, competes with another barber. If suddenly one is given a new costly machine for mass cutting of hair then the whole fabric of society gets affected and money assumes an unnecessary advantage. Take a government servant with a fixed salary. He needs more money because society goes on increasing his desires through marketing and advertising. How to get more money from a fixed salary? He starts looking for alternate sources of money. He comes late, etc., how to handle such workers. Here we are recruiting wrongly, we are unable to give work to people. If we give work only for two hours how can we hold the attention of people and how can we prevent him from working outside.

We recruit people without knowing their characteristics—their *gunas—rajasik, sattvik* or *tamasik.* Or their personality whether *bhakta, jnan, karma, yoga* oriented. Then the leaders themselves have no value system and therefore they do not have the authority over the people.

Take Ravana, he could have very easily overcome Sita but he could never do so. Why? Because the strength of Sita was her absolute purity. It was Sita's moral and spiritual strength because of which Ravana could not dare to approach her.

Today, the leaders, the professionals, the managers have no moral strength and that is why they cannot command obedience and respect from the people. They can only weaken the people by money and pandering to their senses. The example set by the managers and leaders of the society becomes the standard.

Therefore we need Managers who can take pride in Indian ethos, who have self-control, who understand the purpose of life and who strive for self-realisation—Shreshta.

REASONS FOR INDIA'S DOWNFALL

For the last 1000 years we have been slaves of people with no value system. The Britishers wanted to rule over us. They deliberately decided to break-up our education system and our *shraddha* in God and our *dharma*. Instead of our age-old, time-tested, universal values being taught to us in our education system they introduced job skills, clerk making education and they turned us away from our spirituality by highlighting the weaknesses that had crept, in our religion.

It is very easy to keep falling, like a rubber ball down the stairs. To climb up needs effort. The Western cultures are pampering to our weaknesses, they play on our greeds. They have no direction. We have to realise that there is divinity, infinite bliss within us and its manifestation in our life and to realise our true nature is the aim and purpose of all our activities.

This is what we mean by education and self-development.

The calmer we are the less disturbed our neves, the more shall we love and the better will our work be.

9

Teachings from *Shastras* for Modern Management

*Dr. M.B. Athreya**

The word *'shastra'* is an umbrella term covering a wide range of philosophical, religious, scientific and social texts. Examples are the *Upanishads, Ramayana, Ayurveda* and *Arthashastra*. Similarly, the field of management also has wide ramifications. It covers a variety of functions—marketing, manufacturing, materials, finance and human resources; and draws from a range of disciplines—mathematics, economics, accounting and psychology. Some glimpses of the possible lessons from the wide ocean of the *shastras* to the all-pervasive task of management, have been provided here.

KEY BUSINESS ISSUES

Among a wide range of management concerns, there are four

* Management Advisor.

key issues, namely :

- Business and Society interface.
- Managerial Leadership
- Work Culture
- Self-Management

SHASTRA SOURCES

Among the better known sources of *shastra* teaching are the following:

- The four *Vedas—Rig, Yajur, Sama, Atharva*
- The Upa-Vedas—*Ayurveda, Dhanurveda, Gandharva Veda, Arthashastra* and *Kalashastras*.
- The *darshanas* or schools of philosophy, such as *Sankhya, Yoga, Vedanta* and even the atheistic Charvaka.
- Epics like the *Ramayana, Mahabharata* and *Bhagavatam*.
- *Upanishads*
- *Puranas*

BUSINESS AND SOCIETY INTERFACE

Perhaps the central point to note here is that business was seen as a legitimate, integral part of society.

Artha—Wealth Creation

The core function of business was to help the society create wealth through manufacture, domestic distribution, foreign trade, financing and other such related activities. Basham has observed that "from the days of proto-historic Harappan culture, India has always been a trading nation." Exports included jewels, spices, fine textiles, steel, medicines and perfumes.

The *Arthashastra* of Kautilya and the *Dharmasutras* of Brihaspati, Yajnavalkya, Narada and Shukra refer to economic organizations. Of particular interest is the *Sambhuva Samutthana*, a business undertaking in which people joined together, contributing capital or labour, or both. There were provisions for simple and complex partnerships, as well as temporary and long-term ones.

Acquisition of wealth was also recognised as a legitimate human objective. The value was inculcated in children through *Subhashitani shlokas* like "*Kshanasah kanasah cha eva, vidhyam artham cha sadhayet,*" meaning "acquire knowledge by the second and wealth by the penny."

Kama—Material Needs

Business had the role of providing the goods and services to enable people to enjoy another legitimate life objective, namely *kama* or desire for sense enjoyment. Business in ancient India produced and distributed a variety of goods including sugar, edible oil, textiles, pearl, fisheries, ivory, stone, jewellery, furniture, pots and pans, medicines, dairy products and aphrodosiacs. The success of a Raja's rule was partly measured by the range and quality of goods and services.

Dharma—Ethics

Peter Drucker has referred to profit not as the end of business, but as a score of its effectiveness. In ancient India, organizations like the *sreni* (National Guild), *nigama* (City Guild) and *samuthana* (the Enterprise Partnership) were expected to be profitable and viable, but their core objective was *"sarva loka hitam,"* meaning "the well-being of all the people." In the post-capitalist, post-communist world, we are returning to a similar social market economy concept, namely" meeting the expectations of all the 'stakeholders' i.e., customers, dealers, suppliers, investors, lenders, government, employees and owners." The work of business was seen as *'dharma karya'* righteous contribution.

Moksha—Transcendence

An important part of *vaishya dharma,* according to *Arthashastra* was *'dana'*, philanthropy. The banking guilds facilitated donations and gifts for good social causes, such as for the building of dams, roads, bridges; feeding the artisans during famines; and generally helping the needy. Business enabled citizens to move towards *moksha,* by facilitating their going through a phase of satisfying *kama*. The businessman moved towards his *moksha* by serving society first in wealth creation, and later through his philanthropy. This took the form of building schools, mutts, temples, tanks and other such socially useful assets.

MANAGERIAL LEADERSHIP

There are three important leadership roles in modern business, from each of which we can derive useful guidelines from the *shastras*.

The Chief Executive

Modern-day chief executives could draw many useful lessons from the role model of a good raja, as enjoined in Indian scriptures.

- *yatha raja, thatha prajah*—As the king is, so are the people. His values and style influence them.

- *Communication*—Getting frequent reports from his regional administrators and ministers. Also, sending out proclamations and announcements, delivered in the town corners and villages.
- *Hands on*—Travel incognito through the kingdom to verify and correct formal reports.
- *Service*—Welfare of the *praja,* the people, his highest concern.
- *Dharmic rule*—Righteous government. There are profound messages in
    - *Bhishma-Yudhisthira Samvada* in the *Shanti Parva* of the *Mahabharata;* and in
    - Rama's advice to Bharata before setting out on *vanavas,* exile to the forest; among many other such sources.

The Executive

There has been a strong movement around the world for professionalisation of management. This puts a great responsibility on the executives. The core teaching for them from the *shastras* is to follow *shreshtha dharma* or the righteous conduct of the elite.

- *Trusteeship*—a trustee of the resources entrusted to their care—physical, financial and human resources.
- *System Discipline—Yad yadacharati shreshthah, tat tadeva itharo janah*—The conduct, the manner of the elite is followed by the others.
- *Standard Setting—Sa yath pramanam kurute, lokah tad anuvaratate*—what the elite sets as the *praman* or standard is also observed by the ordinary members of the organisation.

- *Harmonising*—The *Shreshtha* must be unbiased and reconcile conflicting pulls and pressures.
- *Candour*—The *shreshtha* must tender good advice, without fear. As Vibhishana tells Ravana,

  Sulabhah purusha rajansatatam priya vadinaha
  Satyasya pathyasya vakta shrota cha durlabaha

  — O king, there are many who will always tell you sweet things. But when it comes to the relevant, helpful, bitter truth, there are few sayers, and even fewer takers.

The Supervisor

Organization of work on sites and workshops was the responsibility of the *Mistri*—the supervisor. His was a respected position and role. Among the guidelines are—

- To be the trustee of skills. The tradition goes back to Vishvakarma, the celestrical architect.
- *Selection*—To spot potential among a number of young aspirants to the trade and stream them into different skill components within that trade.
- *Training*—Guide the apprentices at various stages of work, through supervision, coaching, correction and demonstration. It is remarkable how skills of building temples and forts; metal work; textiles; carpentry and many others have survived for centuries through *Sruti* (hearing) and *smriti* (memory).
- *Tools*—Taking good care of equipment. This tradition is reflected even today in the *ayudha puja* in our factories, or the *Vishvakarma puja*, as it is called in some parts of the country.

WORK CULTURE

In the context of liberalisation and globalisation, this is perhaps the issue of greatest concern to government and industry. *Shastras* have many injunctions to offer.

Task Orientation

There was constant emphasis on work, effort, endeavour.

Udyogam purusha lakshanam

— Effort is the hall mark of human being.

Ma te sangostu akarmani

— Do not be associated with inaction.

Work Standards

Sloppiness and shoddiness were not acceptable.

Yogah karmasu kausalam-

— Yoga is excellence in action.

Excellence has many dimensions, including productivity, quality and service.

Harmony

Avoid destructive enmity and conflict.

Ma vidvishavahai

— May we not quarrel.

Yogah samatvam uchyate

— Yoga is balance. Do not take extreme positions.

Perspective

The word detachment is often misunderstood for fatalism

and resignation. No, our scriptures counsel dynamic action, but with a perspective and without crippling anxiety for results and rewards.

Karmanyeva adhikaraste

Ma phaleshu kadachana

You have control over your action. The end result will be affected by some additional, environmental forces. So, focus your energy on good, competent action. The probability of success will be higher that way.

Discipline

The focus was primarily on self-discipline, and failing that on external discipline

Atma eva banduh atmanah, ripu eva cha.

— The self is the friend, as well as the enemy of the self.

Atmana atmanam avasadayet

— Save yourself by yourself, from destructive behaviour.

SELF-MANAGEMENT

If one were to look for the

- distinctive competence
- core competence
- unique selling proposition

of Indian *shastras*, it is the systematic model of self-management. It has been well recognised that while Western thought focussed more on the external world, Indian thought began with a deep understanding of the self and then related it to the cosmos.

Self-Awareness

The injunction was 'know thyself.' Among several, related answers, are the following enabling, empowering, ennobling ones.

Aham brahmasmi

— I am that *Brahman*, the universal soul.

Tat tvam asi

— You are That, immortal reality of the cosmic universe.

Drives

Understand and moderate your drives. Don't repress them. Allow them scope in legitimate ways. Then transcend them. Further on, transmute the energy of the drives to nobler causes.

Reduce *tamas*—sloth, inaction, negativism, cynicism, fear, anxiety.

Convert *rajas*—raw, aggressive, egoistic, turbulent, energy, into

Satva—refined, highly efficient, focussed, calm, harmonising, socially, binding energy.

Rajas de-energises others. *Satva* triggers others' energies in the right direction.

Strategies

A choice and blend of paths are available. Different mixes are relevant to different situtations.

Karma Yoga — The primary path of workmen and junior executives should be that of action.

Jnana Yoga	Senior and top management needs to provide conceptual, visionary leadership.
Bhakti yoga	Great endeavours cannot be achieved with nagging doubts and disbelief. Faith in the people, their potential; the stakeholders', their cooperation; the society, its ability to resolve contradictions; in human destiny; in cosmic evolution—all these will add to the success of corporate vision, strategic business plans, R & D, investments, globalisation and other such landmark efforts.

Life-Cycle

Graceful transition through the four states of the life-cycle—

Brahmacharya—Scholarship

Grihastha—Householder-hood

Vanaprastha—Disengagement

Samnyas—Renunciation

Some of our family business and corporate succession problems arise from the reluctance of elders to move on to *vanaprastha* and make way for the next generation.

Self-Enrichment

Economics and management science have recognised that—

> Firms have great difficulty in maximising profits. Individuals do not maximise utility.

The *shastras* offer unlimited scope for enriching oneself in multiple dimensions. The self is an ever-expanding set of concentric circles.

- *Annamaya kosha*—The physical body, nourished by the right food is a great marvel.

  Sharira madhyan kalu dharma sadhanam. It is only through a healthy body that one can contribute to the world.

- *Pranamaya kosha-Pranayama*, breath control, is an aid to disease prevention and positive good health.

- *Manomaya kosha*—The mind is a double-edged sword.

  Mana eva manushyanam bandham, moksham eva cha.

  The mind is the bind, and also the release of the human being. So, meditate.

- *Buddhimaya kosha*-Intelligence, discrimination.

  Buddhi nasath pranasyate—When judgement is destroyed, the individual perishes.

- *Anandamaya kosha*—Enjoy pure joy, which can come from a life of awareness, self-discipline, personal growth and social contribution. This is not impractical idealism. In fact, it is the other way round. Neurotic pursuit of success, by any means, in the so-called real world is, in fact, *maya*, the delusion.

This life is short, the vainities of the world are transient, but they alone live who live for others, the rest are more dead than alive. Great things can be done by great sacrifices only.

10

Management: Indian Perspective

*Swami Someswarananda**

Despite learning so many different types of Management theories from USA, Japan and other developed countries, we face many problems in running an industry. There is labour agitation, lock out, sick industry. Why cannot Indian goods compete in the world market? Why are Indians fond of foreign goods? In the changed situation today why are we so scared of the MNCs? And above all, why do we rarely find an MBA among the successful industrialists in India?

What do we lack? The managers in their private talk blame the workers: they are lazy, irresponsible, disobedient! Is this the only truth? Or, are we following out-dated theories and ideas in management?

* President, Vivekananda Centre for Indian Management, Indore.

Management science is based on behavioural psychology. We, at our management institutes, learn American or Japanese methods. Why? Is there no difference between Indian mind and an American mind? Why did Japanese method fail in the USA? The hard reality is that every country has its own characteristics, and unless we note these we will not be able to evolve the Indian method or system. Indian behaviour and the ethos will help us to come out with the right kind of management style.

This appropriate management style will be mentioned as "Indian ethos in management"—Vivek management.

WHY INDIAN?

If there can be British style in management, American style or Japanese style, then why not an Indian style of management? Or to be more specific: Is there any Indian style of management?

When looked in a larger perspective, the traditional Rajasthani carpenters, Gujarati women's skill at handicraft, the wood-carvers of Karnataka show remarkable excellence in their work and production. The Moradabad brassware workers are exporting their products though they do not know the modern concepts like QC, TQM, ISO-9000. How are they doing this? Lijjat Papad, run by Indian women, or the Udupi hotels, are other examples. In management, production, motivation, services, etc., they are showing their excellence. Unfortunately, in industry or management we do not give much importance to these examples in our textbooks. And thus we miss the salient features of Indian style of management.

You will rarely find an MBA in the above cases.

We call this Indian ethos, as the true spirit of indigenous management techniques is expressed in the above cases—by the Indian supervisors and workers. There is excellence in India, and it is better to recognise this hard fact.

We noticed this excellence, searched for indigenous style of management, and then incorporated the concepts of *Vedanta* and *Yoga* to give this a shape. Side by side we experimented with this technique in modern industries, both public and private sector companies, got the feedback, evaluated, and thus a model evolved, the system was perfected.

We call this, Indian ethos in management because, first we learnt this method from the common Indian workers—farmers, carpenters, grocers, artisans, and above all Indian women. And secondly, the Vedantic concepts and *Yoga*-practices were incorporated.

DOES IT WORK?

This technique—Indian ethos in management—was applied and discussed in many companies, and the result was very encouraging. More and more management consultants and teachers are joining this movement and more and more companies are showing keen interest in this.

Suresh Pandit taught and applied this Indian ethos in management in companies like Yash Paper Mill, MTNL, Crompton Greaves, Otis, Buroughs Welcome, Air India, Technova Platemaking Systems, etc.

Prof. S.K. Chakraborthy in TELCO, TISCO, BHEL, BEL, Bhilwara group of Industries, Reserve Bank of India, Oil India, etc.

Mrs. Geeta Patil in Reliance.

Ramesh Seth and Dr. Madhuri Seth in Department of Atomic Energy, Tata Memorial Hospital, ISTD, Johnson and Johnson, Nippon Denro Ispat, etc.

G. Narayan pioneered it at Excel Industries, Yash Paper Mill, etc.

Sunil Kumar of Vivekananda Centre for Holistic Management in IFFCO, Indian Oil, CDOT, Railways, BHEL, Management Associations at Lucknow, Allahabad and Delhi etc. and Sw. Someshwarananda in Indian Oil, Otis, SAIl, Hindustan Copper, Institute of Town Planners, Burroughs Welcom, Tata Consultancy Service, Excel Industries, Taylor Instruments, Railways, BHEL etc.

THE SEARCH

As mentioned before, Indian managers blame the workers for the low work culture and output in Indian industries. But is it realy so?

Is it the only truth? Are Indians lazy? Indifferent? Or, we are following some outdated theories and ideas?

1. So, our search started with a simple question: Is there excellence in India?

And the journey started at our doorsteps. The paper-*walla,* or the hawker comes daily to distribute newspapers. In summer, winter, rain, Bharat Bandh. He comes daily on time—early in the morning. And throughout the year. No Sunday, no casual leave, no bonus, no promotion. Is it not excellence? His case defies Maslow's theory.

Or take the case of the near-by grocers shop. He handles 250 odd customers daily. He knows the needs of every customer. He may not knows your name, but knows where you stay, whether you take Rs.72.20 or 7.85 per kg. rice, whether you like Colgate or Promise. He does not know what is MIS (Management Information System), yet he knows your location rather than your name. He has his inventory, accounts. Just imagine, if a professional company has to handle so many items and more than 250 customers daily, how many departments it would need. How many persons! Ledgers, computers, intercoms... Do we not see the excellence in the grocer's shop?

Visit Moradabad. It is famous for brasswares. They do not know what is ISO-9000, they do not have English-speaking managers. Yet they export all their products.

With so many examples why do we still believe in the American 'stick and carrot' policy? Why do we not look into the real situation, find out some way out which is already in practice?

We go to Japan to learn the 'Kaizen' technique. But have you ever noticed how your wife manages? When you got married, on the first day, you preferred to eat in a restaurant rather than taking food cooked by her. She was a novice then, poor at cooking. But just after one month she improved a lot, and now after one year of marriage you find her no less than any good cook. How could she do this? She never went to Japan to learn kaizen. Kaizen-daily improvement to attain the Zero-defect state-was not new to her.

2. So, we raised another question: How could the same Indians fall into two group— 'lazy, selfish' and Kaizen-practitioner and trouble-shooter? Can we bring the first group to the fold of the second group? An arrogant officer becomes very polite when any guest comes to his house. A lazy typist is very active when there is any cultural show in his office! An 'irresponsible' supervisor takes a lot of trouble to bring up his children!

Thus we see that the necessary quality or the ability is already there in them. The question is : How to bring these out?

3. We started our experiments in different private and public sector companies. One by one companies opened their doors to us, allowed us to go ahead with our experiments. Today we are convinced that a "new approach" is needed to produce the desired result. It is new because in many points it differs with the current practices, including Maslow's. Yet it is not new as it is being practised by many Indians in their own way. We learnt from paper-hawkers, grocers, cobblers, housewives, *panwallas*. We discovered the *Indianness;* the Indian way to excellence, higher productivity, growth, customer's satisfaction, precisely the Indian edition of management and Kaizen.

Based on these experiences and Indian wisdom expressed in the *Vedanta,* a model was evolved, system was perfected. And it produced wonderful results. Experiments were done with many company workers; both in public and private sectors. In Mumbai, Bhavanagar, Delhi, Baroda, Pune, Ayodhya, Trivandrum, Madras and other places the response was very encouraging. Many other companies are also getting interested in vivek-management. Here we shall discuss only the salient features of the these experiments.

4. Our experience is that the workers lack two important things—self-confidence and self-respect. What they need is self-respect and autonomy. Unions did not do much to help them or the industries in the real sense. In public sector, to give importance to concern for workers, concern for customers was neglected. Strong union has made many of them arrogant, but could not inculcate self-respect. Moreover autonomy was never practised as it is the leaders, not workers, who have a voice in management.

Vedantic gospel of "*aham-brahmasmi*" (i.e., I am full of immense potentials) and "*atmanam viddhi*" (i.e., know thyself) played a very important role in our experiments. When we talked to the workers, they thought of themselves as ordinary human beings—a smelter, a fitter, a driver, a crane operator, etc. At the same time, unfortunately many bosses do not want them to have any brain or heart; workers are supposed to follow orders. We asked them "At the beginning was there any difference between my brain and your brain? The discussion went on. Our purpose was to make them self-respected, a dignified human being. It worked miracles. In the present system an extraordinary human being is made ordinary, he does not get a chance to realise his potential. A sweeper is always a sweeper, a typist always a typist, a watchman remains a watchman throughout his life. He is robbed of self-respect and autonomy. Discussion, exercises, role-playing produced wonderful results. They became aware of their latent potentials.

5. Animals need a leader, birds need a master. But do we? A human being can do things himself. Robinson Crusoe is a natural character. At present it may not be advisable to do away with managers. But if we focus on producing self-managing team, this will solve many of the present-day problems.

Before going for that, we must know who will do what. The entrepreneur or the higher management has to create opportunity, he is to produce vision. A manager has to convert this vision into the utilisation of opportunity in terms of a project. Supervisor or the facilitator is to remove the blocks or obstacles; and the result is to be produced by the workers.

Later we shall discuss how a self-managing team can be formed which leads to greater motivation. A leader's role is to play the appropriate role in this process. Once the roles are clear, everyone known what he is to do, the rest will take care of itself.

6. In one such experiment, after the first workshop there were fantastic results produced by the workers. Next month while conducting the second workshop, they expressed their gratitude to the trainer. When he said, "*Ye kam to apne kiya,*" the workers commented,—"Sir, *hamne sab-kuch banaya ye bat to sahi hai, lekin apne hamko admee banaya.*" That is what we mean by self-respect and autonomy.

The workers are intelligent enough to monitor a project or a job. They took care of "quantity" (how much they made—the ideal figure and the actual figures), "cost" (how much they consumed—ideal and actual), (how much time they needed to finish the job).

7. How could we do it? We tried to discover the salient feature of the Vedantic principles, starting from "*Aham-brahmasmi.*" Then from the *Gita* and the *Karma-Yoga* preached by it, we culled some more ideas and put these all in a system. This module helped us to work for the desired result.

Let us, in a nutshell, note the changes brought in.

Present system	*We offered*	*Vedantic idea*
(a) Maslow's theory of needs	Realisation of one's potentials	*Aham-brahmasmi; Tattvamsi,*
(b) Personal gain	Synchronising private and public benefits/growth	*Atmano-mokshar-tham jagat-hitaya ca.*
(c) Man-placement according to academic qualification	Placement according to one's natural inclination	*Jnana-Bhakti-Karma-Yoga*

(d) Individual skill and excellence	Skill and excellence of the team	*Yajna; Parasparam bhava-yantah.*
(e) Hygenic factor	Job-satisfaction through innovation. Making the workers trouble-shooters	*Yogah Karmasu Kaushalam.*
(f) Power-struggle	Giving a more challenging task in another field.	*Moksha*

8. While in most of the cases the "hardware" aspect is given importance (system, structure, skill, etc.) we tried to highlight the "software" aspect. Generally in a training programme functional skill is given utmost importance, we tried to focus on the world-view and the emotional stability of the participants. The difference in the approach is like this:

Present approach **Our approach**

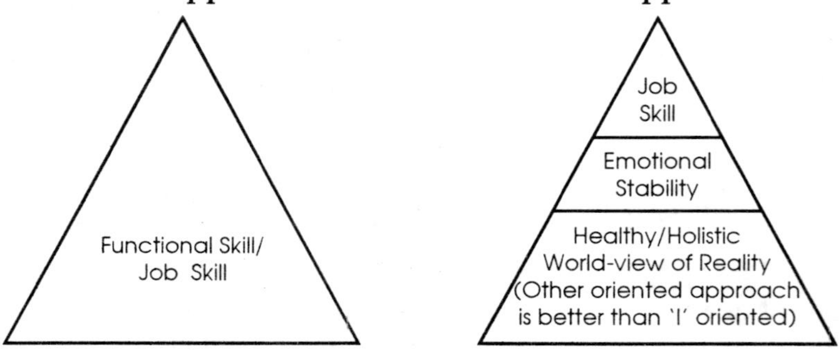

Fig. 1

RE-DEFINE THE MANAGEMENT CONCEPTS

If your actual knowledge-experience-skill is 'X'; and the knowledge-experience-skill you apply in your workplace daily is 'Y', what is the difference between 'X' and 'Y'? Vast difference! You can contribute much more than what you are doing now; you could achieve much more than what you did so far. The things you learnt from books, the nature, from life, from others—if you add all these, you will realise that your actual strength is much more than what you think of yourself. Your brain, is a supercomputer, the ears are a part of fantastic stereo-system, your voice and eyes can challenge any audio-visual system made artifically. Once you start making proper use of these, these will work miracles.

This is what the *Vedanta* teaches : *Tattvamasi* (You are That, i.e., you have immense potentialities). And so also do your subordinates. What is needed is *Atmanam Viddhi*—know your actual strength.

This leads to a better management concept—productivity in terms of people's capacity is much more important than productivity in terms of plant capacity.

But what is management? Not just "getting things done by others," but "helping ordinary persons to produce extraordinary results."

Does Maslow's theory really help in motivating people? If you are a supervisor or an assistant manager, you cannot give an extra increment or monetary benefit to your subordinates (as this is the job of the top management). It means you cannot satisfy the physiological needs of your subordinates. Moreover, according to law there is no permanent job because job is a contract between two parties which can be terminated by any of the parties with prior notice. So, how as a junior manager will you satisfy the security need of your subordinates? But you have to motivate them. How will you do it? The *Vedanta* says : *'ananda'* and 'freedom' are the goals everybody is trying for. Now, if you allow your subordinates more autonomy and make them more creative, they will get more motivated. We will not discuss these methods here just now. We could evolve the exercise and modules in this regard and apply them in many industries. The results was fantastic. In one company, the workers went for record production though no manager guided them in their day-to-day work.

Job-enrichment is also another debatable concept in spite of Herzberg's hygiene factor. Can I always get a job of my liking? Moreover, why do I always depend upon external stimuli to get myself motivated? Transactional Analysis is somewhat right, but why should I always need a positive stroke? In this real world, if I always depend on positive stroke or external stimulus, it will make me psychologically dependent. What is needed today is "mind enrichment." Can I make any job, whatever I do, interesting? And that is what *Vedanta* teaches—this is *Karma-Yoga*. This is what a housewife practices unknowingly.

Again according to *Vedanta*, *"Sukshma"* (subtle, subjective) elements are more powerful than the *"sthula"* (gross, objective) factors. What is the significance in management?

First, inner resources, (courage, insight, foresight, etc.) are most important than external resources (land, labour, capital). Second, profitability in terms of good image, credibility and people's trust is more important than profitability in terms of money. If a company made a profit of 10 crores of rupees last year and this year the profit is 12 crores, does it mean that the company is doing well? Not at all. May be because of government budgetary policy the company could make more profit, or may be that because of price hike it could make more profit though it sold less numbers of products this year! Moreover, if you like to buy shares of that company, will you go by the balance sheet it presents? Certainly not. So, balance sheet or profit in terms of money is dubious.

Religion teaches us to be people-oriented. As Swami Vivekananda suggested, Buddha advised, Guru Nanak, Kabir, Christ, Mohammed and others taught—A people-oriented balance sheet:

1. Number of customers—Loss/Gain in the number of customers.
2. Average turnover per customer.
3. Number of negotiations in hand (last year and this year)
4. The stock of contracts (for both years)
5. Analysis of the target group (what percentage of market the company could make its customers—their profile)
6. Prospective customers—(i) in the existing market; (ii) in the untapped market.
7. Degree of satisfaction of the customers.
8. Degree of dissatisfaction of the customers—Dissatisfaction in which area?
9. To what extent is the infrastructure of the company strong enough to double its customers service?

It is a common sight that one who has shown excellence in his company, fails miserably as a parent in his house. The problem is that in management training the participants are considered as managers only. The teacher forgets that a participant is not only a manager but also a parent, a friend, a relative and above all a citizen. Unless all these aspects are integrated, training will remain incomplete and one-sided. And that is the crux of the problem today. The *'advaita'* (non-dual) concept of the *Vedanta* asks us to see the person in his totality.

From this concept we can go to the next corrolary—in management training we should give importance not only to the intellect but also to emotion and action. FIRO-B, MAO-B, T-P, leadership questionnaire, etc., are fine, but only intellectual understanding will not help. *Vedanta* suggests the path of *jnana, bhakti* and *karma*. One is to coordinate (*yoga*) the intellect (*jnana*), emotion (*bhakti*) and action (*karma*). In training programme we first involve the participants in discussion (this helps them to grow intellectually and be creative). Next we prescribe some techniques of mediation to translate the intellectual concept into the feeling level and to remove mental blocks. And thirdly, we show them the action-steps. Thus when these three - *jnana, bhakti* and *karma* - are integrated, the learning gives better result.

Job-hopping is spreading like cancer. Employers complain that the people are no more committed to their organisations. But if money is the sole criteria, this is bound to happen. Actually the problem is - work/job is considered as a means to earn money. Unless a higher philosophy guides the people, the scenario will not change. So the basic question is - Why work? Vedanta made it very clear that work is a means to grow. The *karma-yoga* preached by Sri Krishna and Swami Vivekananda highlighted this idea and explained it at length. Unless there is a deeper meaning of work, nothing will work. Indian wisdom suggests an alternative concept than the prevailing Western concept. According to Indian ethos, effective supervision is to supervise the growth of the people (subordinates) in their workplace. More autonomy and creative opportunities will make them not only more productive, but also highly motivated and committed.

In motivation two things are important. First, how a manager can motivate himself inspite of all obstacles. This self-motivation is the most important factor. And secondly, how to motivate the subordinates. Today it is not motivation but "inspiration" that is needed more.

In marketing, the focus should be more on 'problem-solving' rather than 'satisfying customer's needs.' It is very difficult to differentiate between need and want. Do you really need one soap for soft skin, another soap for oily skin? Does one really need a TV set which provokes his neighbours to pelt stones at the TV set? Though in management books 'need' is highlighted, in practice the companies stress on 'want.' So it is better to stress on problem-solving of the customers or the people.

Competition does not help much. What is the use of marketing a similar product just because it is selling? Problem-solving standpoint helps a company better. India is a vast market and it is still untapped. Farmer's footwears, electric generator for poor householders, safe and less expensive gas cylinder, etc. are still not available in the market, yet luxury goods flood the market. A company competes because it does not have the self confidence which can make it unique.

To take class on system, the teachers still harp on the cybernetic method which is basically the hardware aspect of a company. Inspite of all precautions, a system may fail if the people running the system, are not good. In politics, presidential system succeeded in USA while it failed in African countries; in Britain the parliamentary system flourished but in Pakistan it did not work much. It is high time we give more importance to the software aspect of a system. We like to redefine 'system' like this " A system is a particular human response pattern expressed through the organisational functioning." How to analyse a system and make it more effective?

Instead of going for a structure which is working well for another company, it is better to have organic evolution. If the purpose is to help or solve the problems of the customers, the structure has to be adequate to serve the purpose. So it is better to start from the last point i.e. customers. Health of a company does not depend upon its productivity or economy but on one point - how best it can solve the problems of the customers.

ISO-9000 is being practised by many companies but it is a painstaking job to implement it. However, if we concentrate on our immediate supplier and customer, the process will be much easier.

Seva AND PROFITABILITY

The concept of profitability in terms of money is wrong. It is misleading. In the religious scriptures it is always emphasised that "*sukshma*" (subtle, intangible) is more powerful than the "*sthula*" (gross, tangible). If we interpret this in the business—language it will be like this—profit in terms of good image of the company, customers' trust, social attractiveness (all intangible factors) is more important than profit in terms of money (tangible factor).

"OTHER" VERSUS "I" ORIENTED APPROACH

A basic wrong concept prevailing in the business world is that by being more self-centred a company can make itself more secured. And thus they are trying to develop an all-round defence against the changes in the deficit factor. Even departments like R&D and HRD are not there in most of the companies.

Now this sort of all-round defence, as it is practised today, is backfiring because this is an I-oriented approach. And because of this approach, which is basically wrong, there is uncertainity in the business world, there is tension, anxieties, worries, meaningless stiff competition, back-stabbing , etc. To solve this problem some businessmen are trying to please the political leaders, another thread—pulling tactic—which is corrupting the electoral process; at the same time the business world is suffering. This self-defence process based on I-oriented approach is basically wrong. (See Fig.2)

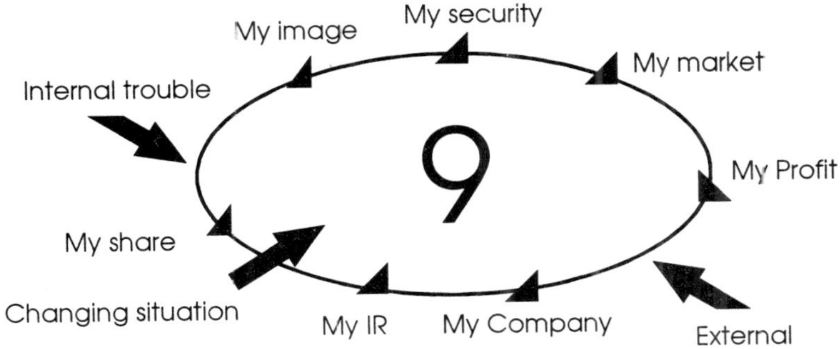

Fig. 2

The real self-defence system can be built up when one takes other-oriented approach. There is basically a wrong concept that selflessness is an ideal and not practical answer to the hard reality. Unfortunately people do not notice that helper is the real beneficiary. Between a teacher and his student the teacher may not pass but the teacher get his salary. Between a doctor and his patient it is again the doctor who is the beneficiary because the patient may or may not get cured but the doctor will get his fees. Regarding the joke about Indian crabs (a crab when tries to come out of the can, is pulled back by another crab) it can be said that if the second crab helps the first one to go out the second crab also comes out in the process. That is why Swami Vivekananda said "you get benefited when you help others."

The real power is not the capital or knowledge or skill or any other thing. The scripture says *"sanghe skakti kaliyuge"*—in the *Kaliyuga* power is in organisation. The real power is with the people. How many people are with you—that is your real strength. A director, in terms of knowledge, authority, designation is much higher than the Union leader, yet the Union leader is more powerful because he has more people with him.

How does other—oriented approach gives better result? See Fig.3.

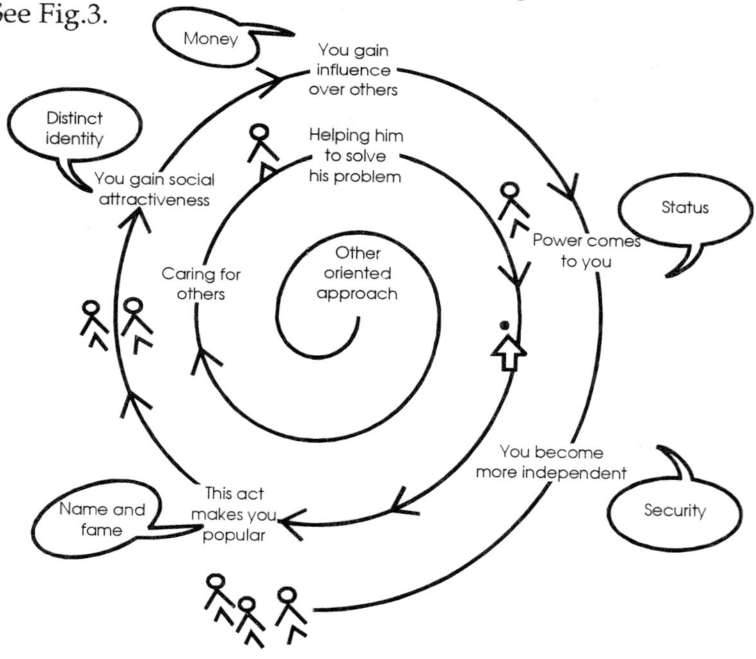

Fig. 3: Other Oriented Approach

Balance-sheet, as we see it today, does not reveal the true picture of a company. It shows only a part—financial aspect—of the company though it is very much misleading. And that is why one does not go by the balance sheet of a company when he buys shares.

Yajna AND GROWTH

Your organisation runs smoothly when the workers play complementary roles to each other. Similarly when your organisation plays a complementary role to other organisations in the society, it runs smoothly. Acting against the society or other people does not work for long. Organisation faces uncertainity and stress in the process; ultimately the society hits back just like nature. Environmental pollution, deforestation are just two examples. Lord Krishna in the *Gita* emphasises that work should be done in the spirit of *"yajna"* and *yajna* means *parasparam bhavayantham*—nurture each other.

Growth is an automatic organic process in which simple materials and energy are united into higher systems. Growth comes when a company does, in its own interest and on its own initiative, that which is in the interest of the society or people. It is in this goal that the personal interests of a company and the interest of the society meet. Any other criterion of growth is suspicious and unreliable. The purpose is to make the external forces (product, people, companies) as friends and helpers. From a confrontational attitude one has to turn into a peaceful hand-in-hand cooperation between one's company and the society.

So the point is to synchronise the private and public benefits. The more closely a company concentrates on the basic need of a target group in the society, the better it solves its own problems.

CHECKLIST

Here is a checklist assigned to help you to know whether your company is on the path suggested in this paper.

1. Does our product/service fulfil any basic need of the

society?

- Is this solution quantitative or qualitative?
- What is our solution offered to the customers?

2. In what is our company specialising - product or solving a basic problem?
3. Are we competing with any company?
    - Why?
    - If 'Yes', then in which area?
4. What is the special strength of our company?
5. In which area is our company unparallel?
6. How can we diversify our role-playing complementary role in other areas?
7. What image of our company does the society have?
8. How many entrepreneurs from our employees could the company develop during last three years?
    - How can we intensify the process?

1. Do the people need our product/service badly? Why?
2. Are we prepared to allow the public to check our accounts?
3. How to make our product/service the best and the cheapest?
4. How many negotiations are in our hand now?
5. What is the stock of contracts?
6. How many customers do we have this year? Has the number increased or decreased than the last year?
7. What is our average turnover per customer?
8. What does the analysis chart of our target group indicate?

What percentage of customers are we serving?

What is their percentage in the existing market?

How can we increase the number?

9. Who are the prospective customers?—
   - in the existing market, and
   - in the untapped market?
10. To what extent the customers are satisfied with our product/service?
11. What is the degree of dissatisfaction? In which area?
    - Do I know the officer/staff well? What is his special strength? What makes him different from others?
    - Is he in the right job? Has he the necessary resources?
    - Does he really know the other team members and the organisation?
    - Is briefing regular? Does it cover current plans, progress and future developments?
    - Do the team members know what standard of performance are expected?
    - Does he know how his work contribute to the overall result?
    - Does he have sufficient authority for his task?
    - Has adequate provision been made for training or retraining both technical and as team member?
    - Is he growing? Does he see the chance of development?

- Do I spend enough time with individuals listening, developing, counselling?
- In which area is the leadership now (growth/ crisis)?

Swami Vivekananda in a letter dated 1.8.1898 wrote:

"Any amount of theoretical knowledge one may have, but unless one does the thing actually, nothing is learnt. I refer repeatedly to election, accounts and discussion so that everybody may be prepared to shoulder the work. If one man dies, another—why another only, ten if necessary - should be ready to take it up.

Secondly, if a man's interest in a thing is not roused, he will not work whole-heartedly. All should be made to understand that everyone has a share in the work and property, and a voice in the management. This should be done while there is yet time. Give a responsible position to everyone alternately, but keep a watchful eye so that you can control when necessary; thus only, can men be trained for the work.

Set up such a machine as will go on automatically, no matter who dies or lives.

We Indians suffer from a great defect, viz., we cannot make a permanent organisation—and the reason is that we never like to share power with other and never think of what will come after we are gone."

Life is short: Give it up to a Great cause. Arise! awake! and stop not till the goal is reached.

11

Managerial Insights

*Sunil Kumar**

IDEALS OF WORK

On the quality of our aim in life depends the quality of our life. We are what our thoughts are. Doing is very good, but that comes from thinking. Fill the brain, therefore, with high thoughts, highest ideals, place them day and night before you and out of that will come great work.

Motivating the Man in the Manager to work for his self-development

What are we all working for? What is our purpose in life? Knowingly or unknowingly we are all working for the attainment of the highest ideal of perfection. This perfection is already within us. It is our real nature. It is a state of limitless knowledge, happiness and life. The question is:

* GM, The PEC of India Ltd.

How can we work so that whatever we do brings us the realisation of that perfection within us? Manager must work in such a way that he will manifest more and more of his inner perfection through his work.

Managers are leaders of men. Whatever a leader does, people follow

If the Managers adopt for themselves a higher set of ideals; develop a visionary purpose in life and a missionary zeal in action, then the entire organisation becomes surcharged with effectiveness. What is the ideal of work placed before us? Each Manager is potentially perfect. The goal is to manifest this perfection within. Do this by work (or by knowledge, or worship or control techniques, by one, or more, or all of these) and be free. This then is the ideal of work; to attain the highest perfection through work and be free. This perfection within is presently disturbed by our actions and its consequent reactions. The question is this Is our daily work at war with this perfection? How can we work so that whatever we do, brings us the realisation of that perfection? This '**How**' is the subject of *Karma Yoga,* the philosophy and science of work, which should be studied, practised by every manager. This is the science which we have inherited from the *rishis.*

The responsibility for the effectiveness of organisations rests with the **Level of Development** of the individuals who run them. The development of the individual to achieve the development of the organisation is necessary and it really means developing the Man in the manager.

> The *problem of low productivity in India is jealousy.* "Three men cannot act in concert in India for five minutes. Each one struggles for power and in the long run, the whole organisation comes to grief."

As per Vivekananda's analysis, India's thousand years of slavery and political imprisonment has generated this quality in Indians; just as it has for others who have experienced similar servitude. The solution lies in surrender to love and discipline throughout management and the workforce. Indian managers need to return to *sadhana*; to turn to specific practices for developing themselves since all management is finally subjective.

Management is decision-making

Decision-making has always been, is always and shall always be, in the ultimate analysis, *subjective*. 'Learning to be' is thus more important that merely 'Learning to do.' In 'Learning to do' it is the intellect that develops. But the intellect is merely an instrument and not the subject. The intellect has a sharp eye for methods and tools, but is blind to ends and values. It has powerful muscles but no personality. It should be made to serve the subject, not lead. 'Learning to be' needs practical techniques for self-development (*sadhana*). It needs knowledge of the aim and purpose of life (philosophy of *Vedanta*) and understanding of how to work (science of *karma yoga*) so as to reach the highest level. Managers, as leaders of men, need to have a higher purpose in life, something towards which their whole life can be directed, which will give meaning and direction to their work. What better purpose can there be than to strive to manifest the inner perfection through work; this alone will bring prosperity to the organisation, society and the individual.

Indian Managers' poor contribution to Team Work

People 'working together' for achieving 'common objectives' constitute an organisation. The higher the common objectives of the organisation and the higher the values and ideals of its managers, the greater is the commitment of the workforce.

Conversely, the lower the objectives and ideals, the lesser is the commitment.

In spite of having the highest ideals and techniques for self-development why has India failed? Why are managers cynical, lacking faith in themselves and therefore unable to delegate and build up team spirit? To a large measure because the so-called educated managers are blissfully ignorant of the fundamental issues, that is, the aim and purpose of life and the role of work in achieving them and have therefore no *shraddha,* no intellectual conviction of the ideals of work placed before us in Indian philosophy. What are these ideals? In essence these are :

1. Work is *yajna;* the 'giving' of a hero and not the 'taking' of a beggar for, it is 'giving' which maintains the world.
2. Work for *chittasuddhi;* purity, filling the mind with happiness and peace.
3. Work is worship; is to be done with dexterity so that the inner divinity, which is pefection, is manifested.

If we work together for achieving this 'common objective', the organisation and its workforce will prosper.

Creating a Training and Development Oriented Organisation Culture

The more knowledge you give the more you get. This is a universal law. Thus, the more the efforts the senior managers make in imparting their knowledge and skills, in developing their juniors, the more they will gain experience. This chain reaction leads to organisational growth and expansion.

Any intervention to change or development of organisation culture should come from the top with total faith and commitment. HRD is an important intervention.

Unless the top and senior management put their heart and soul into training and development and is totally committed to it, these interventions will have no impact.

It is up to the senior managers to first be inspired towards undertaking self-development programmes for themselves and then inspiring and motivating their managers and helping them to grow and develop.

Training and development does not merely mean going on a training programme but this means a continuous, daily, deliberate effort to improve oneself. This is not easy, so we have to always be on the lookout for inspiration and help.

Science supports the Indian Thought

Ever since 1893, when Swami Vivekananda proclaimed to the world the glory of India, of her *rishis* and of her *Vedas*, the eternal message and wisdom of India has spread far and wide and truths contained therein have influenced the greatest scientists and thinkers of our times. Every advancement in science has, as it were, taken place only to reaffirm that there is but one reality. The very difference between the subject and the object has now disappeared into the holistic unity, the new vision of the interconnectedness of everything, the one reality now being acknowledged by the modern scientists, which is but the eternal message of the *Upanishads*.

The modern educated India, however, continues to be unaware of the wealth of knowledge contained in the *shastras*, knowledge which can be harnessed for not only the material and scientific progress of the nation but that which can be harnessed for self-development, for our own prosperity.

Value of Work

Work we must, values are no substitute for hard work. But values give direction and add flavour to the work and give it an altogether new dimension, a profoundity which converts work into worship.

What is the essence of Indian thought as applicable to the managers? Very simply stated, it is:

> Each manager is potentially perfect and the purpose of life is to manifest this perfection within. This perfection can be achieved through work itself if we have the right perspectives and perform the work with the right attitudes.

Instead of just working, without a higher purpose, if we spend sometime in seeking answers to some fundamental questions, it will help us in being excellent managers. It will give our work a sense of direction and the work will acquire a new meaning.

What are these fundamental questions?

Who am I? Who is the man behind the manager? Who is the person who sees and perceives the objective world? What is our mind? What is our intellect? Who am I? What is the universe? What is its purpose? What is relationship between me, the work and the universe?

Why Values?

Management is decision-making. Decision-making has always been, and shall always be, in the ultimate analysis, subjective. The training and the purification of the subjective, the Man behind the manager is, thus, imperative for effective decision-making.

Having a set of values and ideals as our guide and practising daily the techniques for self-development, *sadhana* gives us that all-important subjective quality that may be called **Character Efficiency**. Its results may not be immediately perceived but nevertheless it ultimately leads to individual and organisational effectiveness. If not apparent in the short-run, most certainly it will always show in the long-run.

It is our duty to determine our purpose and mission in life. We may have many goals to achieve but the purpose of life is something higher, it is the road we decide to travel on. Goals are mere milestones on this road and we should avoid treating goals as the purpose of life. The purpose of life is an ongoing, continuous process and requires a long-term vision and corporate leaders have to be men of vision.

It is up to the managers to improve the image of India, bring back our pride in being Indian as-much-as in Indian goods in the world markets.

It is a universal law that whetever a leader does, people follow. Thus, managers, as true leaders of the workforce of the nation, must lead the way and adopt for themselves the highest philosophy, the highest values and ideals and the best techniques for self-development available. The work-force will then follow suit and the nation will then prosper.

What are the gains of having a manager motivated with the highest values and committed to self-development?

He becomes creative and innovative, a team-man, a productive and efficient worker.

In short, a manager is one who believes in the ideal given by Swami Vivekananda, "Ask nothing, want nothing in return. Give what you have to give, it will come back to you, but do not think of that now. You have the power to give, give and there it ends. Learn that the whole life is in giving."

Education and Training

These are meant not only to give us knowledge and information, which alone the present systems provide, but also to build up our character, for which we have not yet made any provisions. We need a set of values and ideals as our guides and self-development techniques so that we can make the values a part of our character. The words and examples of men who have lived such ideals give us the inspiration to strive for it. The education and training programmes must therefore cater to this need and if not at the school or college level then at least the professional organisations must do it for their manager's families.

LEARNING TO BE

It is now recognised the world over that training "To Do" is not enough. Learning "To Be" is now the keyword. What are you is equally, if not more, important than what you do. Thus, a new dimension for training and HRD needs to be added. We certainly need tremendous work efficiency, knowledge and translation of knowledge into action, but along with it we must also have character efficiency. Then alone we get total human excellence.

India has specialised in investigating and discovering the profound divine depth within a man. Man—the object, is the focus of attention of the modern world and its physical sciences; but Man behind the manager; Man, the subject; Man, the knower; as distinct form the known, is the science of spirituality which is a more challenging study than the study of objects. In this science, India has forged ahead and the message of the *Upanishads* is astonishingly profound. By discovering the immortal in man and in nature, the *Upanishads* made themselves and the Indian Vedic Culture immortal. This knowledge must be regained by the managers if we want to bring India back to its earlier position of glory when India was the leader of the world.

Managers as the leaders of the workforce should study these aspects and develop their own behavioural sciences based on the messages of the *shastras*. These insights into the behaviour of people from the *shastras* have a lot to contribute for motivating and developing India as an industrial and scientific nation. It will be good if some research work in this field can be initiated.

NATURE OF WORK

By the very nature of things we must all work incessantly. And all work by its very nature is composed of good and bad. Good and evil both will have their results, will produce their *karma*. Good actions will entail upon us good effect; bad action bad and both will bind us. What then is the solution? The solution reached, in regard to this bondage-producing nature of work is, that if we learn to be a witness to the work we do, it will not have any binding effect on us. These ideas of the science of work, *karma yoga*, need to be thoroughly discussed and understood—since we all have our own misunderstandings. Through constant study, analysis, reflection and *sadhana*, we move towards clarity of vision. But first we should have *shraddha*, faith in the values and then we should ask questions to clear out doubts and seek to understand.

The philosophy of *Vedanta* and the science of *karma yoga*, perhaps are the foundation of the Indian management culture, Indian management ethics and Indian work culture, which we the professionals have to usher in, to rediscover it, to imbibe it and to spread it in our organisation and make it our guide in our daily life.

Need for Ethical and Spiritual Values

The year 1967 started with an All India Colloquium held in Mumbai on this subject under the chairmanship of Dr. K.M. Munshi, President of Bharatiya Vidya Bhawan with Dr. R.R. Diwakar, Chairman, Gandhi Smarak Nidhi, and Swami Ranganathananda of the Ramakrishna Mission as co-chairman and with a highly distinguished galaxy of leaders like the then president, Dr. S. Radhakrishnan, Vice-President Dr. Zakir Hussian, Shri N.H. Bhagwati, V.C. BHU, Shri M.C. Chagla, Dr. C.D. Deshmukh, Shri V.V. Giri, Shri V.K. Gokak, V.C. Shri Morarji Desai, Shri K.C. Pant, Shri H.M. Patel, ICS, Shri C. Subramaniam and many other luminaries of our country as members, many of whom are amidst us even now.

THE GENESIS OF THE COLLOQUIUM

Ethical and spiritual values can only provide a sure basis for a creative social order on a firm basis for the integrity of India.

It was noted that presently education places too much emphasis on imparting knowledge and too little on building of character and assimilation of necessary social, moral and spiritual values, specially the spirit of service.

The problem identified as early as 1967 has not been tackled at all by our so-called leaders of society and the situation today is still worse!

Confusion with religion and secularism, is adversely affecting Indian work efficiency.

Each person is potentially divine; is potentially perfect. This is a universal statement applicable to every being of the world. The duty of every person is to strive to realise this. For all of us who are working, our work is the means by which we can realise perfection. We should therefore learn what is the correct way of work and practise it at our workplace.

This attempt to realise our divinity is religion. Each person is unique and he needs a different technique for becoming perfect. The process is not easy. We need help at every stage and more important we need inspiration. This is the purpose of the founders of different religions, the great spiritual teachers. They come from time to time to guide us. Their lives and their teachings are always simple and straight-forward.

In the name of secularism, we deny our children exposure to the lives and teachings of saints and sages of every religion. Instead of saying that religion will not be taught it would be better if every person from school upto his professional qualification is exposed to the best of every religion and is inspired and motivated to seek his own answers, understand the spirit of the scriptures and adopt healthy techniques of self-development. Done openly and with freedom, every religion has the power to inspire its adherents to strive to be perfect. The superstitions, the evils which are imposed on religions by narrow-minded, selfish, power hungry so-called religious leaders can be exposed by making study of scriptures and their teachings open, free and compulsory for all people.

Manager as a leader

It is the managers who have to take up this leadership because they are the leaders of the workforce of the nation. It is because the educated people have stopped reading the scriptures and seriously practising its teachings and understanding its essence that the petty-minded, self-centred religious leaders have grown. Each of us, must know our own and two or three other religions well and above ali we must have an environment where we sincerely strive to develop ourselves.

If the management training programmes are conducted in selected Himalayan Retreats (not hill stations, please) and the philosophy and science of work imparted to the managers then the people can be inspired and motivated to strive for perfection through work.

The very presence of the Himalayas will awaken in the manager feelings of grandeur, strength, fearlessness, infinity and respect and reverence for the highest and free them of petty-mindedness. This is the eternal power of the Himalayas. The setting of the Himalayas and the knowledge of the ideals of work and the techniques for its practice in our daily life and work, will help our workforce manifest the twin ideals of work placed before us, *tyaga* and *seva* as well as the zeal to do, whatever they do, perfectly. This will be true individual and organisational effectiveness.

Mere work efficiency of the West, without character efficiency already stands exposed as a failure. Mere commercial interests of the organisation without holistic and long-term vision and ignoring the environmental needs as practised in the West has already caused us enough damage.

VALUES

The conflict between what we want to do and what we should do is resolved depending upon our own value systems. We may accept truth as a value but when in a crisis, whether we stick to it or not depends on how deeply the value has become embedded in our character. How do we imbibe these values in our character? An old Sanskrit saying says "Man knows *dharma*, but does not practise it. He knows *adharma*, but he does not desist from it." There is also its Biblical counterpart. "The good that I would, I do not; the evil that I would not, that I do."

It is only due to the fact that we have no intellectual conviction of the values. In most cases, we only know by hearsay that an act is either right or wrong. If we knew it ourselves and it was self won conviction, we would never have deviated from the right path. Our fault is really not so much a lack of will as of lack of direct self-acquired knowledge. In day-to-day life, the knowledge of a fact, as a rule, leads us to action whose aim is the positive one of securing something we like or the negative one of avoiding something that we dislike. Self-effort to realise these values is also many times treated as a value, but these are instrumental values, not ultimate values. Thus, money is an instrumental value, while the satisfaction of life's need to which it is the means can be an intrinsic value.

Apart from the universal values common to all, there are certain values which are the characteristics of a nation. *tyaga, seva,* tolerance, contentment, simple living and holistic vision come to mind when we talk of Indian values; cut-throat competition, commercialism, advertisement and materialistic interests are certainly not Indian values.

TWO FUNDAMENTAL ERRORS IN THE WESTERN THOUGHT

Why bother about the Indian values in management when the West is known to be more industrially advanced? Should we not bring in the Western values for better work efficiency? These and associated questions need answers. The Western models are already crumbling and their values systems are based on two fundamental and gross misconceptions. Firstly, man originated from monkey and, he is now getting more and more civilised and secondly, that there is only one life of 50 to 70 years in which all inequalities between people have to be explained and, equality established.

On the contrary, the Indian insights assert and prove that the first few men were the greatest *rishis* and not monkeys and that we are the descendants of *rishis*. Secondly, people are not equal, and this inequality has to be respected and accepted and our effort should be on the growth of man and not to make him equal to others. He is a higher man who can lift others and it is the duty of all men to help others grow.

DESIRE, DUTY AND VALUE

What concerns each one of us personally is our desire. What does not concern us personally but concerns other persons and things in our life is duty. A set of values helps us to shift from mere fulfilment of desires to learning to do our duty. The *Gita* is the solution to the conflict between desire and duty. Understood thus, the question becomes one of finding out what is ours and what is not. It is a complex question. It is this confusion which is clarified in the *Gita*.

Conflict arises because there is another urge from within which does not reconcile with duty. This is because we are not very clear in our minds about our duty. There is something we intuitively recognise as our own without any doubt but when we deal with others we start using logic. All arguments arise only in respect of others.

It is this confusion between what is mine and what is not mine which leads to a conflict between our desires and duties. Indian values based on Indian philosophy, which emphasize that there is but one reality, that there is none other than myself, solves this conflict.

Sanatana Dharma UNIVERSAL VALUES

Though we call it Indian values, in actual fact, these values are universal values, eternal principles and are universally applicable to all human beings whatever their country or religion—*Sanatana dharma*.

It is, of course, a matter of fact, call it coincidence if you will, that these principles were given and nurtured in this land, now called India. So, what we call the Indian values are in actual fact applicable to all people. These values are based on the insights and truths discovered by the *rishis* for the benefit of all people. It is these insights, these fundamental truths, which are the real foundation and backbone of Indian culture and, in fact, of all religions of the world, which are but attempts of man to become perfect.

This *striving by man to become better till he becomes perfect is religion*. Thus, religion becomes a must for everyone. Different people need different inspiration and methods but as long as they agree that becoming perfect and better persons, is the purpose of religion, then it is possible to extract, the best ideals, from all religions for each age group. Then we should see to it that these universal values are taught to each child throughout his educational period. He would thus grow into a better person with a sound value system and learn to take decisions which are good for both people and organisations. Instead of highlighting the differences, let us identify and follow various points of agreement. Every sincere effort of a man to know the truth, become a better person and deal effectively with others and realise the truth at work, is religion.

Sanatana Dharma means eternal values, *Vedas* means knowledge. The terms are universal in nature—there is no sectarian view and no narrow divisions involved. They apply to all people. These principles are the foundation of all religions, and must, therefore, be understood by every manager, because they are the leaders and they guide the vast workforce of the nation.

Essence of Indian Ethos

(a) Each soul is potentially divine.

(b) The goal is to manifest this divinity within by controlling nature—external and internal.

(c) Do this either by work, worship, psychic control or philosoply, and

(d) Be free.

(e) This is the whole of religion. Doctrines, dogmas, rituals, books, temples or forms are but secondary.

—*Swami Vivekananda*

This simple but essential message and purpose of all religions, that is, each being is potentially divine (perfect) and that its manifestation is the goal and our work is our opportunity to manifest this perfection within needs to be clearly understood. The essence of different religions needs to be culled out from their scriptures and placed before everyone so that all of us are familiar with the other man's path to perfection and all of us grow into responsible citizens and workers. This can only be done by educated and intelligent people and cannot be done by power hungry politicians or narrow-minded and ignorant, so-called religious leaders.

RESPONSIBILITY OF MANAGERS

How can we, the managers as a group of educated people, take the lead in seeing to it that as organisations we help in developing responsible citizens and workers? Perhaps, by making the study of true religion fashionable once again amongst educated people, so that superstitions and fanatical views now held by people in the name of religion can be exposed as a fraud being played by narrow-minded and orthodox religious leaders for the sake of money and power. They succeed only because they keep knowledge a secret, they form narrow groups and because we, the educated people, have made no efforts to understand what religion means. Everyone of us must *strive to become better*. And this is as much needed at work as in temples and churches. Therefore, managers have a responsibility towards religion by providing the right environment at work places.

IDEALS OF WORK AND INDIAN INSIGHTS

This is based on *Karma Yoga* of Swami Vivekananda.

What are the highest ideals of work placed before us?

The goal: Isolation of the subject, the knower from all objects, from anything known or knowledge, mental and physical, is the goal. When this is attained, the subject will find that it was alone all the time, and it required no one to make it happy. As long as we require someone else to make ourselves happy, we are slaves. When the *purusha,* the Man behind the manager, finds that it is free and does not require anything to complete itself, then freedom is attained.

Everyone must work, but what matters is how to work and in what way one should work. Men run after a few dollars and do not think of cheating to get those dollars; but if they would restrain themselves, in a few years they would develop a character that would bring them millions of dollars—if they wanted them. Then their will would govern the universe. If we work with proper understanding, then our work itself becomes the means for freedom. If we work without understanding, then our work leads to bondage and misery.

Work in freedom and not as a slave

The man who works in freedom and love, does not care for results. But the slave wants his whipping: the servant wants his pay.

It is extremely difficult to work for work's sake. This is the ideal. But people always have some motive for work. If it is not money, it is power. If it is not power, it is gain. Somehow, somewhere there creeps in a motive. You are my friend and I want to work for you and with you. This is all very well, but take care, you must agree with me; if you do not, I shall no longer take care of you. This kind of work for a motive brings misery.

Bliss is found when we work without expectations of any rewards, without any motives, as masters of our own minds, and not slaves to our motives.

Working your best in the situation you are placed

We should stop grumbling and cribbing about our environment and the situation in which we are placed. The situation is not in our control, but our reaction to it is under our control. Let reaction to the situation be a considered action; for we will be judged by how well we act in the situation. Therefore, every situation is under our control, if we learn to 'act' in it properly, rather than grumbling and 'reacting.'

Working without a motive

A good worker concentrates his whole self in his work and he loses all other consciousness for the time being. But people are able to do only a single job perfectly at a time. Thus the ideal is that all work should be done. Striving for perfection, in whatever duties one has to perform, is the means which helps us realise the ideal, that is, perfection and freedom.

Right Attitudes to Work

He who is one with the Lord through *yoga* performs all his work by becoming immersed in concentration and does not seek any personal benefit. Such a performance of work brings only good to the world and no evil can come out of it. Those who work thus, never do anything for themselves. This is the ideal. Striving for perfection in whatever duties one performs, doing it with utmost dedication and total concentration, without expectation of any reward or gain, unattached to the results, to the best of one's ability is the means of realising the ideal. It is this attitude to work which has been found to be most inspiring for us in India. It is the duty of the managers, as leaders of our workforce, to study and understand these ideas and practise it themselves. The workforce will then spontaneously be inspired to adopt these ideals. This is the self-motivation which must become a part of our work culture. It was this striving for perfection in life through striving for perfection in our work that had brought India its glory when people from all over the world flocked to India not only for spiritual wisdom but for its excellent goods and above all its wealth. All may not be able to practise the ideal yet, but for that reason the ideal cannot be lowered, it still should remain as the mission of every worker and it is this common mission which is the unifying factor for true individual and organisational effectiveness.

The Law of cause and effect

Every thought, word and deed brings its reaction. A good thought, word or deed will bring happiness and an evil thought, word or deed will bring misery. This is the universal law. Each action will have its reaction on oneself and none can stop it. It, therefore, follows that if I am happy it is my own thoughts and deeds which are responsible and similarly, if I am not happy, I alone am responsible. Therefore, the solution has to come from within. To work without motive, to work unattached brings the highest bliss and freedom.

Work, but let not action or thought produce a deep impression on the mind. This can be done if we remember that *the whole of nature is for you, the subject; not the subject for nature.* The very reason of nature's existence is for the education of the subject; it has no other meaning. It is there because you must have knowledge and through knowledge you free yourself. If we always remember this, we shall never be attached to nature. We shall know that nature is a book that we are to read, and that when we have gained the required knowledge, the book is of no more value to us.

Be a Master, Not a Slave

The whole gist of *karma yoga* is that you should work like a master and not as slave. Ninety-nine per cent of people work like slaves and the result is misery; it is all selfish work.

Work through freedom; work through love. Love is very difficult to understand; love never comes until there is freedom. There is no true love possible in a slave. If you buy a slave and tie him down in chains and make him work for you, he will work like a drudge, but there will be no love in him. So, when we ourselves work for the things of the world as slaves, there can be no love in us, and our work is not true. As we do not ask for any return from our children for the work we do for them, similarly we should expect nothing in return when we do any work for a particular person, a city, or a state.

If you can invariably take the position of a giver, in which everything given by you is a free offering to the world without any thought of return, then your work will bring you no attachment, which comes only when you expect a return.

If working like slaves results in selfishness and attachment, working as masters of our own mind gives rise to bliss of non-attachment.

All thought of attaining return for the work we do hinders our progress; and in the end it brings misery.

WHY INDIAN SHASTRAS FOR MANAGERS?

This art and science of work, has been understood and explained in India in great detail, but, not being followed because, the educated managers and professionals, are ignorant of the high ideal. The adverse unseen inner effect which every work leaves on our mind is because work is not done with the proper skill of being desirelessness in action. Brought up as we are totally under Western influences; we have like them, kept money and power as our ideals of work and do not even know of the high Indian ideals of work.

We must remember that the values and ideals of work, as practised in the West, based as they are on money and profit as the end and ultimate aim of life, have already been exposed as a total failure. The environment problems it has created and the exploitation of natural resources it has encouraged, where 6 per cent of the world population gobble up 40 per cent of the worlds resources has already brought the world to disaster. The West is realising it and is now looking to India for a solution. International best sellers like Schumacher's *Small is Beautiful*, Hazel Handerson's *Alternative Futures*, Fritjof Capra's *Turning Point, Eternal Wisdom*, etc., clearly point to a shift towards Indian insights.

Indian insights thus, cater to the root of our personality. They give us the intellectual conviction that the ultimate aim and purpose of work is perfection and freedom and not money or profits. Practice of unselfishness is the path to the goal and not selfishness. Once this subject is attended to, the 'ability' will come easily and better performance will come. *"It is good and very grand to conquer external nature, but grander still to conquer our internal nature. It is grand and good to know the laws that govern the stars and planets; it is infinitely grander and better to know the laws that govern the passions, the feelings, the will of mankind."*

Long-term view, creativity, intuition, sound decision, calmness, contentment, peace, sense of joy in work, freedom from stress, strain and tension, team spirit, working for the good of the people, unselfishness, determination to complete the work, capability to negotiate on the basis of win-win situations, conviction in the power of good, capability of chosing the long-term good, eschewing the short-term seemingly pleasant; all these qualities and many more will come to the managers who take the trouble to understand Indian insights.

HOLISTIC VISION

Indian society has a very great and glorious background and its thought has reached and effected the entire world.

Today, however, we find that for some reasons India is not in the forefront. It is, therefore, necessary to look back and find out what was it that made India a great civilisation and then use it for our managerial practices.

If we look into the *shastras*, we find that they have clearly understood human behaviour and interactions and have *dealt with all the complicated problems of life with very consummate skill and consideration.*

The top most, modern scientists are now realising that they are perhaps dealing with things, which are only peripheral and they have not yet been able to go deep into the essential!

A fragmentalised approach or compartmentalised approach to any problem is bound to lead to incomplete and incorrect theories.

Therefore, it is only a holistic view and approach which can give us a satisfactory solution, whereas a part view can never give the correct solution.

"Doing is very good, but that comes from thinking . . . Fill the brain, therefore, with high thoughts, highest ideals; place them day and night before you; and out of that will come great work.

12

Management to Vivekmanagement

*Sunil Kumar & S.K. Palhan**

Considering the growing menace of selfishness, corruption and inefficiency in our organisations and managerial processes, there is a need for a change in the way we manage. The change should be towards a harmonious blending of modern management skills and knowledge with the age-old, time-tested universal values and eternal principles—Vivek Management (VM). The modern TQM movement also supports the introduction of basic values and people focus in management. Indian ethos offers universal values, work ideals, systems and organisational structures which we need to adopt in our managerial processes. Instead of just management let us adopt Vivekmanagement as the Indian management style in our business and society. VM means

* Professors at Sri Sringeri Sharada Institute of Management.

managing through wisdom based on lofty values and work ideals and with focus on meeting the needs of people.

At the outset let us note that the TQM movement also follows the same lofty values and clearly accepts that *organisations exist in society to fulfil the needs of society* and that *profit is our compensation for service to society*. Therefore service to society is the cause and the means as well as the purpose of individuals and organisations and profit is only an effect and not the goal. Unfortunately, because of our job-skills-career oriented education system and our society's insistence on promotions as a yardstick for progress, everyone looks for individual gains and profits. Our existing Indian Institutes of Management or our educational systems provide only job-skills but nothing on character building and understanding and managing oneself and of Indian values an ideals. Indian ethos want us to realise that character building is the foremost task of education and *karma yoga* should be our work ideal. If we have team spirit and a serving and helping others attitude as individuals and as business organisations then profit will come to us and we do not have to seek it. To get an intellectual conviction in this, we need *viveka*, the power to discriminate the right from the wrong and the strength to traverse the critical path to the goal. Our education, therefore, must give this conviction and our management system must support it as it is the key even to profitability, excellence, quality, etc., as the TQM movement has brought out. In fact, TQM asserts that unless people are intellectually honest, self-controlled and have respect for others we cannot achieve teamwork without which we cannot become world class. These values must be brought in our TQM and HRM practices and it must be the grounds for promotion to senior position.

MODELS OF MANAGEMENT EXCELLENCE BASED ON PEOPLE MANAGEMENT SKILLS

Mr. Peter Hutton, Director, Mori UK, a specialised niche-market research organisation was in Mumbai advising companies like Mafatlals, Godrej, Bombay Dyeing, etc. (ET 10-4-96). He has carried out an extensive external audit of employee attitudes and internal communication systems to understand the shortcomings in terms of services provided by the employees to the customers and the service demanded by the employees for themselves.

Mr. Hutton has put up, *'Employee loyalty as the new corporate mantra for nirvana.'* Mr. Hutton has explained that his object was to help corporate houses to build models of management excellence and understanding the key issues of people management. He has rightly pointed out that people are ultimately the key to any business. Crorporate houses must understand the need to evaluate them properly. They must use all expertise to develop better intra-personal skills and to communicate to people their aims and objectives in a loyalty-inspiring way to meet the growing challenges of competition. He goes on to say that most surveys have shown that salary is not the driving force behind retaining people. Work atmosphere, leadership, management style are in effect more important.

VIVEKMANAGEMENT MODEL FOR MANAGERIAL EXCELLENCE

All this is true. We must focus on people. But, when it comes to people we must remember that in the entire modern management practises, people are treated as a tool for production—Human 'resources' like other material resources. Are people just resources for better production of results? Are modern organisations not interested in the 'growth' of people to *nirvana*? This is where we offer the VM model based on Indian wisdom. Improved individual productivity and organisational effectiveness are guaranteed if we use VM principles and VM model. Even in todays' business world whenever some enlightened organisations have agreed to use this model it has immediately shown quantum jump in results. It is based on how Indian people behave and their values and ways of managing. As far as people management is concerned let us remember that Indian ethos offers the best ideals. India has always been and is even today the spiritual *guru* of the world and if the world has any respect for India of today it is only because of its spirituality. Among the Fortune 500 top organisations, most have been there for a long, long time and are well-known for their reliability, intellectual honesty and strong value system.

In fact the Western countries are more honest today, transparent and straightforward in their daily business dealings than the land of *satyamev jayate*. Generally people are honest and want to be honest but it appears that our systems are such which discourages honesty and is not conducive to trust and respect for each other and encourages satisfying the boss rather than serving the people. Let us see how a typical Indian, who is not a part of this modern Western culture and management, runs an organisation. See the *bania*, the tailor, the washer man, the craftsmen. These are examples of typical Indian organisations. There is no boss, no central planning, no purchase manager, no director, etc. Each is a self-managed team directly responsible for results and for serving the needs of customers. They just fulfil a particular need and by that wheat grown in north reaches the *bania* shop in the south. Imagine if we hand over this to the modern, educated organisation. We have to be thankful that only 8 per cent of the workforce is in the organised sector whereas the balance 92 per cent of the workforce is working on simple Indian system, e.g., Bombay lunch boxes, delivery systems of newspaper, Uduppi Hotels, etc., We have to learn management from common Indians and not Western management institutes. We need a change from management to Vivek Management.

THE CHANGE FORMULA

A good manager is defined (UK) as one who initiates and implements changes and continuous improvements. For this we need *vivek* to decide what to change and its direction. Is there a need to change? To analyse this issue let us take the help of the 'change' formula which states the conditions for change: **A+B+C>R**, i.e., for change to take place **A+B+C** must be greater than the natural resistance to change; where A =Dissatisfaction with present, B=Shared vision of future, C=Agreed first step and R=Resistance to change.

Dissatisfaction with present (A) [A+B+C>R]

In 1947, India was considered among the top 10 developed nations and had about 5 per cent share of the world trade. Today we are below 100 and less than 0.5 per cent respectively. There are over 33 lakh sick units, Rs. 115,000 million is blocked up in just 2.5 lakh sick units and 25 per cent of banks resources are blocked in non-performing assets. The thousands of crores in PSU's and the government enterprises have all failed to produce effective results and are squandering public money and are unable to fulfil the needs of people. No group of employees is happy, people do not trust each other. We are educating and choosing our managers with great care and promoting them on various performance appraisal systems (instead of the character roll) and yet we are getting only self-centred, selfish and greedy leaders. Hardly any organisation has developed unique products and none is able to offer world class engineering goods at competitive prices in any field. With the MNC's coming, in the era of liberalisation, privatisation and globalisation, we will soon reduce back to an agricultural economy unless we are able to improve our work culture and productivity. We are wasting our time and money on policing, supervising, monitoring and have no time for innovation, design, research and improvement. So we remain copycats and hence second graders. We learn and teach motivation, leadership, team building and a host of managerial tools but very few managers are able to motivate and give the leadership to get the best out of the people. Our systems are not-responsive and work culture is poor. Thus, there is a unanimous agreement on dissatisfaction with the present state of affairs as has been the feedback in the numerous programmes that have been conducted. If we all agree that the present systems are not satisfactory then the question arises, what should be the shared vision for future and the agreed first step? Do we Indians have a shared vision of future? Is it the same as of others?

Shared vision of future (B) [A+B+C>R]

Values: Let us examine the aim and purpose of life, the role of work in achieving it and how our work and management can help in our growth besides producing effective results. The first question is why only Indian wisdom? Because it is based on the holistic vision of the *rishi's* who were selfless sages interested in guiding us on the critical path to the goal. The present systems are given by self-centred people with limited vision and therefore cannot guide us. Management is based on how people behave and the people of different nations have different values and behaviour patterns. Thus, the Britishers had their own style, the Americans developed theirs and so did the Japanese. What about Indians! India could not have been a leading nation in world affairs for thousands of years without a very strong, well developed education and management system of its own.

The *Mahabharata* war was fought by over 47 lakh soldiers with about 14 lakh chariots, 20 lakh horses and 4 lakh elephants. All these had to be fed, clothed, accommodated and since all were killed in just 18 days they had to be disposed off also. Daily 2.6 lakh men and 1.2 lakh animals were being killed. Imagine the management skills, systems and organisational structures which achieved it!

Therefore, let us not learn education and management only from the West. Let us also look into our own values, ideals and systems and harmoniously blend both to offer a Vivekmanagement model to make India face the challenges of globalisation. Swami Vivekananda has said that the Indian work ideals are *tyaga* and *seva;* our national ideal is spirituality. Indians love and respect a *tyagi* and not a *bhogi*. *Karma yoga* is our ideal. The aim and purpose of life is to achieve infinite perfection because that alone is a state which can satisfy our quest.

Action is inherent in the nature of man but all actions bind man to reap the consequences of his actions and this keeps him in a perpetual cycle of bondage. *Karma yoga* is that skill in action by which work does not become the cause of bondage but becomes the opportunity for our growth towards infinite joy. It is for the managers to study this work ideal, understand it and set up systems which are conducive to its practice. Third chapter of the *Gita* deals with this ideal.

The life and teachings of Shankara, Vivekananda and other masters provide us the inspiration and knowledge for self-development. In the book *'HRM & Indian Scriptures'* brought out by the Ahmedabad Management Association,

Swami Paramananda Bharati has clearly brought out the concept of work which when done as *yajna* to help the society helps to refine our character. A unique feature of Indian ethos is that the society, individual and business and the relationship between them have been clearly defined based on the holistic vision of the *rishis*—the concept of oneness and the feeling of *apanapan* with more and more people.

The essence of the values given in the scriptures and expressed in the life and teachings of Shankara, Vivekananda and others should become a part of our HRM and education system. It is the managers who are the fabric of society and are, in fact, the leaders of the vast workforce of the nation. As leaders, managers have to remember that whatever a leader does, whatever aims and values he has, the people will follow and people will become what they aim for and what they hold on to. It is, therefore, up to us to develop a shared vision of the future based on the Indian ideals.

Epics like the *Mahabharata,* and *Ramayana* are essential Indian Management Textbooks all of which advise to work for *bahujan hitaye, bahujan sukhaye*. The concept of *moksha*—freedom, a state of infinite everlasting bliss is the ideal placed before us and can be achieved through our work if we apply ideals. Work means daily interactions with people, decision making process, managerial process, and if all these are directed for serving others then we can become better and better and grow towards inifite joy through our work itself.

Whenever we strive for excellence, do our duties and help others we are on the path to the goal. The higher the shared vision of future of any organisation the more it will help in its prosperity and growth and it will be more long standing. Therefore Indian ethos offer lofty values and work ideals as our shared vision of future. Gradually we have to struggle to reach the ideal. Through *dharma,* earn wealth, enjoy and be on the critical path to the goal, is the essence of Indian ethos.

The glory of Indian organisations in the past and how they have been destroyed: In contrast to the present uncompetitive state of the Indian organisations and workers let us look back to ancient India when people flocked from all over the world to partake in her glory and grandeur and for loot and plunder. People did not come to India because Indians were poor and workers were lazy and inefficient. They came to India because Indians offered unique products. Indian workmen were the world's best artistes, craftsmen, carpenters, ironsmiths, goldsmiths, weavers. India produced the world's best textiles, ships, architectures, irrigation system, mathematics, astronomy and so on.

It is the fault of our present-day management systems that we are unable to tap the full potential of our people. Indian organisations were based on small self-managing groups who were directly in touch with the customers and thus were able to meet the "needs" of the people. Indian workers were the best in the world and even today Indian professionals and workmen are the most highly paid in the USA! We therefore need to examine and compare our existing systems with past ones.

Textile Sector: In his description of *Ancient India,* Thornton describes, "A busy population had covered the land with marks of industry, skilled artisans converted the rude products of the soil into fabrics of *unrivalled* delicacy and beauty. Architects and sculptors joined in constructing works the solidity of which has not, in some cases, been overcome by the evolution of thousands of years. The ancient state of India must have been one of extraordinary magnificence."

A Historical Disquisition Concerning Ancient India by Robertson records, "In all ages gold and silver have been commodities exported with the greatest profit to India." The Roman empire had banned trade with India for they feared that once the trade started, Indian goods would become so popular that India will take away all the wealth of the Roman Empire by offering its unique products! India became rich and prosperous by developing unique products and selling it for gold. The art of spinning and weaving was very much advanced in ancient India. The Greek word for cotton textiles *'Sindon'* is derived from *'sindhu.'* The famous muslim cloth of India is known in Greek as *'Gangatika'* from the Ganga and calico textiles is derived from Calicut, the south Indian port which sent cloth all over the world.

To sustain the Industrial revolution of Britain, the British destroyed the weaving industry of India and the consequent blocking of hand spinning leading to the ruin of handmade textile and thus the entire Indian economy. Along with it they destroyed the roots of the *self-managed-organisations concept of Indian ethos in management*. The British also broke down the traditional Indian systems of education (*gurukula*) and health (*vaidya*). In 1931, during the Round Table Conference in London, ***Mahatma Gandhi criticised the British for breaking down the beautiful tree of Indian systems and exposing its roots to die and decay,*** instead of nurturing it and allowing the beautiful tree to grow up. For destroying the Indian textiles industry in order to ensure the sales of British textiles the weavers were subjected to severe tortures. They were prohibited to work in homes and were forced to work only in the East India Companies' factories. They were treated as 'slaves' and to avoid tortures, had to resort to cutting off their thumbs. British workers were brought to India to enable them pick up the secrets of the Indian excellence. The British parliament were deeply involved in developing the strategy to sell British textiles to India and destroying the Indian textiles industry. Sir Thomas Munroe who was in India for 28 years, in early nineteenth century, reported to the Lords Committee:

"Those articles which he (the Indian) wishes for his food his own country supplies, all the clothing it supplies in much greater beauty and variety than anything we can furnish him with. I never knew a native who did not have a large piece of coarse woollen of their own manufacture. *It is so much cheaper than our manufacture, that I am afraid our woollens can never come into competition with it.* They are fully competent to supply all demands that can arise among themselves and that the chief cause of the difficulty of exporting our manufacture to advantage for sale in that country (India) is that *we as a manufacturing people are still far behind them.*"

About Indian worker he says, "Are not the people of India more sober and diligent and as much employed and skillful in manufacture as the inhabitants of any country you are acquainted with? *There can be no human beings more patient, or more industrious, or more sober than the Hindus* and deriving their knowledge of the arts from the object immediately before them."

To kill the Indian industry and to force British goods on India they imposed very high tariffs on Indian manufactures and no duties on their imports. Sir Martin states, "for over a quarter of century we have compelled the Indian States to buy our goods. Our woollens are free from tariffs. Our cotton textiles are charged only 2 per cent tariffs while we have imposed on Indian goods, the tariffs from 10-100 per cent, 500 per cent and up to 1000 per cent. I do not think it is a trade benefit. It is the power exerted by the strong over the weak. Export of our famous Dhaka muslin amounting to

Rs. 3 million in 1787 were completly stopped by 1817 and by 1821 all exports of Indian silks was banned.

As Sh. R.C. Dutt points out in the *Economic History of India*—"deliberate attempts were made to use political power to discourage Indian manufacture from being sold even in Indian markets so as to allow sales of the British textiles. *"The cottage industry of India had to perish in order that Lancashire might flourish. The Indian shipping had to perish so that British shipping might flourish."—Gandhi.* Thus India which in the eighteenth century was producing rich cloth and other consumer goods of topmost quality throughout the country in thousands of villages (SMT) was by the end of century exporting raw cotton and other raw materials and importing cloth and other consumer goods. *Her flourishing cottage industries were destroyed, her prosperous villages were devastated and her affluent, dignified and free people who were serving the needs of people were doomed to poverty, humiliation and slavery.* As Gandhi lamented, "We committed a crime against Indian humanity when we parted with the spinning wheel and sold the economic independence of India for a pottage of foreign cloth."

Organisational Systems: It may be noted that *India's golden age and immortal civilisation, can be attributed to two fundamentals: Vedanta (knowledge) and small self-managed organisations based on hereditary work skills, for example,* weaving, *vaidya, gurukula,* etc. *Vedanta* offers the unique *Indian world-view of oneness* where the focus is on the subjective, the knowledge that we are one, instead of the Western world-view of "Separatedness" and its focus on the objective which is manifold.

The small self-managed organisations were more in the nature of families and network of families scattered throughout every village, which could directly meet the needs of the people. For them work and home were 'one' and not 'separate.' For them, 'society was God and work was service to God in form of society. Work was worship. Work was not to get promotions, or for profits. Work and business were opportunities to manifest our divinity by using our skills and knowledge in the spirit of *tyaga* and *seva* for fulfilling the needs of people. Work was *yajna*. Man is bound by shackles of *Karma* only when he does the work for profits. But when man performs work in the spirit of *yajna*, for the good of others, then such work does not lead to bondage.

Therefore, one should efficiently perform ones duty, fearlessly and free from attachments, for the sake of *yajna* alone. ***This is our shared vision of future.***

Agreed First Step (C) [A+B+C>R]

Uptill now our Management Institues and HRM have been imparting only management skills but through them we have failed to tap the full potential of people. We now need not just managers but *vivek* managers having the intellectual conviction that work is also an opportunity for growth. The Agreed First step is therefore to implement the VM model for improved individual productivity and organisational effectiveness (Please see the case studies). VM lets performers work and think for themselves based on self-managed VM teams networking together with payments linked to results and no pyramid of advisors and controllers bossing over the performers who are to be trained and empowered and given the freedom (creative joy) to produce results. The seniors are to focus on their functions of visioning, innovation, design, research, etc., and creating systems "which can provide the people the maximum scope for refining their *samskaras* (tendencies) through their daily work life and become nobler and nobler".

Sh. V.R. Gowrishankar, The Administrator of Sringeri Muth, while conveying the benediction of Jagadguru on the inauguration of Sri Sringeri Sharada Institute of Management Vasant Vihar, New Delhi, has stated that a good manager is one who understands human mind and how we react differently under different circumstances and conditions. Our work and our managerial processes must help us achieve the ultimate objective of a peaceful and contented life for all beings. The success of organisation will depend on how it develops the available human resources and what systems and structures are created so as to blend all resources towards the ultimate objective. Our ancient culture and ethos give us a background on how this could be achieved through our work. Dr. M.B. Athreya has said that Indian ethos offer growth model for a balanced persuit of multiple life objectives and how the surplus is to be shared and experienced.

TRAINING OF VIVEKMANAGERS

The best age for inculcation of good values is 0-8 years and one should start on the process of self-development, *sadhana*, for growth by age of 8 years. Perhaps in our HRM processes we could inspire the employees as parents to focus on these aspects themselves and also for their family. We have to understand that through our HRM processes the agreed first step will be:

> *Understanding the world-view of oneness, oneself, mind, etc.; the role of work and business in achieving the goal of life; the critical path to the goal and developing the viveka and strength to traverse the critical path.*

HRM people have to become the spiritual *gurus*. As per the best seller, *The road less travelled* (Scott), the following lessons are necessary for growth; how to delay gratification (*tyaga*); knowing what one is responsible for (*karma*); dedication to truth (*dharma*, i.e., the critical path) and balance (even-mindedness so that one can take fair and just decisions). Self-development would include prayers-meditation, reading of good books—life and teachings of saints, etc. We must inspire managers who want to be leaders to strive for self-development, for then only can they inspire others. The Indian ethics are very clear that what the leaders do so shall people follow. Therefore these values are a must for managers who have to deal with people and are the leaders of the vast workforce of the nation.

Organisational Systems (VM): The world over a lot of work is going on to find better ways of managing people in organisations and achieving better results. Re-engineering and corporate restructuring are the key issues. Tom Peters in his '**Liberation Management**' has brought out the need for small self-managed organisations. The quality circles concept and TQM movement has also brought to focus the need for small units in direct customer-supplier mode.

In India, management consultants like Dr. N.H. Atthreya, Suresh Pandit, G. Narayan and corporate leaders like Mr. K.G. Shroff of Excel, Mr. Jhunjunwala of Yash Paper Mills, Mr. Chandra Prakash, M.D. of M/s Fixwell, Sunil Kumar GM, The PEC of India and others inspired by Swami Jitatmananda and Swami Someshwarananda, have done a lot of work to evolve the Vivekmanagement model. The experiments relating to MTNL, Air India, Yash Paper Mills have received wide publicity. (Please see the case studies).

"Oneness"—Apnaapan: VM principles guarantee success because they are derived from the Unique Indian World-view of 'Oneness' given by the *Vedas*—the holistic vision of great *rishis*. Understanding this concept, reflecting upon it,

achieving *shraddha* in it and striving to feel it through *sadhana* are the essential *steps* to peace, prosperity and joy that we seek from our managerial processes. A man with an ideal may make thousand mistakes but a man without an ideal is likely to make tens of thousands mistakes. Thus, the ideal of oneness—a state of infinite joy, is necessary in our education and HRM. The individual, the organisation, the society and the ideal are all interconnected and therefore work and business are our opportunity to grow towards oneness.

The idea of exploiting nature or others through business arises only because of our ignorance of this concept of oneness or lack of intellectual conviction. In our organisation the owners and all employees are 'partners' and if they work together, give better productivity and service to society and justly share the surplus then that is VM in practice. Management and workers are not 'separate.' The union is there to 'unite' them. Today everyone operates from the world-view of 'separatedness' which results in perpetual confrontation and conflict because each wants to preserve his 'separatedness' rather than merging it into the 'oneness' of infinite joy. In the concept of oneness everyone is conscious of his duties and knows that if he does his duty well then alone will he get prosperity. In the world-view of 'separatedness' we talk of our rights and demand our rights even without doing our duties. If all owners and employees are 'one' then the job of each is to help the growth of the other. It is the particular responsibility of the elder, the more maturer and *'viveki,'* to help the growth of others. If all employees are one then it is not a question of finding faults but of identifying the strengths of each and together offering our best skills to solve the problems of society. Work is our opportunity to grow so as to feel oneness with more and more people. This feeling of oneness is the real 'promotion' and sign of growth and progress. Such managers will be able to produce performers, and create systems which are conducive to growth of all.

CONCLUSION

We have seen that all people are dissatisfied with present managerial systems and that there is an alternative, the Vivekmanagement model which offers a lofty shared vision of future and implementation of VM is the Agreed First step for improved individual and organisation productivity leading to national welfare.

Professionals like Doctors have already been made legally accountable to society for results. We the Management and educators are responsible for the selfishness, corruption, poor work culture, sickness and inefficiency in Indian organisations. Before the public and the court realises it and starts shouting for our blood let us resolve to start using VM model. Let us study the VM model, adjust, adapt and refine it and help evolve an Indian Management style which can not only produce world class results but also help in the growth of all.

- *Life is short; Give it up to Great cause. Arise! awake! and stop not till the goal is reached.*

Let positive, strong, helpful thoughts enter into their brains from very childhood. Lay yourselves open to those thoughts, and not to weakening and paralysing ones.

13

Ethics in Management

*Swami Tattwajananda**

MANAGEMENT

The art of management is as old as the human civilisation. It is, what, why and how of things an administrator does. The Industrial Revolution developed the concept of a manager whose work is to conceive, design, develop, produce, market and deliver products. The primary objectives of management, in words of Peter Drucker are: Survival; Growth for fuller enjoyment; Profitability. These objectives created go-getter, rib-digger managers looking for productivity, profits and promotions by hook or crook. This kind of intelligent utilitarian management brought in "moral horrors and spiritual agonies" again in the words of Peter Drucker (in his new book "The New Realities").

The Japanese (Matsushita and others) learning from

* Ramakrishna Mission.

American failures, in the post-war era, added some values like national service through industry, fairness, harmony, cooperation, etc. But once the stage of striving for economic growth is over the purposelessness is driving Japanese to a similar situation; the number of mental health clinics is on the rise in Tokyo.

Hence in Management circles rethinking has set in to find new strategies for better human response in increasing productivity and profits through introduction of ethical values.

ETHICS

Ethics in the West is originally derived from Greek ethos. Greek Philosophy, mostly speculative, aims at freeing the mind from the bonds of ignorance and tries to remove the fear of unknown by presenting the world as something accessible to reason. Disinterested enquiry itself is ethically good and forms theoretical basis for totality in practical life. After 2000 years of development the basic principles of Western ethics to judge human conduct are: Right, Good, Ought. A right action tends to bring about what is *good* for many and a person *ought* to do it. Conscious mental process called *motive* which includes *desire* and *intentions*, with a determination to act, that is, will, brings in an action. This will, depends on habits, that is, character, is strong where single universe of desire dominates and must necessarily be related to an ideal. Hence ideal in life, and character are important.

IDEAL

Ideal of human life is based on concept of Man. The Western concept of Man in Judeo Christian tradition is "born sinner," in Greek tradition "Political Animal," in Socialist thinking

"Social animal," in Techtronic America "Tool making Animal," in Freud's opinion "Biological Entity" and in the words of Alvin Toffler "Economic Animal." Naturally Western ideal of man more or less keeps us in the world of animals.

According to Indian sages of yore, Man is divine and his ideal is to unfold this divinity within by controlling nature, internal and external. Man born like animal is raised to human level through education and to divine level through spiritual training.

Any organism seeks fulfilment. This is the end and aim of all its activities as maintained by modern biology. In the *Upanishads* we have the beautiful concept of freedom *(mukti)* and fullness *(purna)*. Man wants to become integral and experience the delight of freedom, to enlarge the bounds of his awareness, to get *bodhi,* complete enlightenment as the Buddha expressed it, the great aim of human evolution. Education, culture, socio-political processes, religion, business, are meant to increase and enlarge the bounds of human awareness and the range and depth of human fulfilment by increasing our knowledge of and control over not only the outside world but also the deep releases within ourselves. Knowledge is power in positive science. it is more so in the science of *yoga* and it is higher in terms of quality.

This ideal of, Divinity of human beings, oneness of Universe and the process of *yoga* was proclaimed successfully to the world by Swami Vivekananda at the Parliament of Religions a hundred years ago.

Atman is the constant behind the changing body mind complex. It remains unchanged through the three states of experience waking, dream and dreamless sleep and through birth, growth and death. *Brahman* is the constant behind the changing nature. It remains unchanged through birth, growth and death. This *atman,* i.e., Man and *Brahman,* i.e., God are one.

By its very nature *atman* is *sat chit ananda* which is man in the real sense while the apparent man has death, ignorance and misery. Human evolution is meant to elevate the human mind from its attachment to the apparent to its realisation of the real.

ETHICS IN INDIA

In the *Vedas, Samhitas* talked of *ritam* and *rinam* cosmic order and man's obligation to the order. *Upanishads* and *Gita* developed two concepts on basis of the above. (1) *Dharma* (2) *Karma.*

(1) *Dharma* is the primary principle supporting the universe and is also the philosophic speculation based on empirical experience about the absolute. Basically it states, what helps man in establishing kinship with fellow creatures is good and it shows a way how to do it. Four *pramanas* or proofs are given about what is *dharma*:

   (a) *Shruti—Upanishads*

   (b) *Smriti—Gita*

   (c) *Achara*—Life and teachings of men of realisation like Sri Ramakrishan.

   (d) *Atmatushti*—Conscience of a properly disciplined mind, pure and righteous.

(2) Every action is *karma* and it brings reaction in course of time. A human being who doesn't reach life's fulfilment has to take rebirth. As you sow so you reap. The present is the result of past actions and future can be changed by adjusting actions in present.

Every *karma* leaves *samskara*—impression on mind and secondly brings in material results—*karmaphala*. These two(*samskara* and *karmaphala*) combined seeks a person just as a calf find out its mother out of thousands of cows, so says *Mahabharata*. Hence past *karma and self-efforts are considered two wheels of this chariot called body whose horses are the senses, reins the mind, charioteer the buddhi and owner the atman*.

Unless conscious of your own *prakriti*, the *gunas, sattva, rajas* and *tamas* that constitute your psyco-physical set up, lead you to various *karmas*. It is important to note that all education and training is meant to raise man from *tamas* dullness to *rajas* activity to *sattva* balance, finally transcending all three.

So one can see that Indian Ethic of *dharma, karma* and *gunas* is much more comprehensive and includes Right, Good and Ought.

MORAL VALUES AND *Purusharthas*

Based on these Ethical values Indian sages, many of them busy kings, developed the following moral code to be followed by all.

1. *Dama*—self-control
2. *Shraddha*—self-respect
3. *Swadhyaya*—self-effort
4. *Satya*—truth
5. *Asteya*—non-stealing
6. *Vidya*—knowledge
7. *Dhee*—wisdom
8. *Brahmacharya*—sexual purity
9. *Ahimsa*—non-injury

10. *Shaucha*—cleanliness
11. *Akrodha*—freedom from anger
12. *Seva*—service to all beings

Secondly the two secular *purusharthas* or paths to reality wealth (*artha*) and pleasures (*kama*) were subordinated to moral conduct (*dharm*) and realisation (*moksha*).

HUMAN RESPONSE DEVELOPMENT

Ego management through self-control

The Indian managers are considered egotists. They usually follow two rules of management. (1) Manager is always right, (2) If he is wrong refer to rule no. (1).

However one has to be objective to be successful where one judges a situation in which one is placed, as an observer, reducing chances of being carried away by untrained emotions.

This is achieved through self-control. The senses are powerful horses but maneggiare (originally meaning to train a horse in his paces) needs to direct them at his will. Communication of the intelligence with cosmic intelligence through meditations brings in purity of *buddhi* turning it into *medha*. It can't take wrong decision. Sexual purity controls passions and turns it into higher emotions like love and concern for all.

Rajasya mulam shasakasya indriya vijayam. (Chanakya). One who controls onself controls all. Then only regionalism linguistic bias, caste conflict, religious tensions will cease.

Ayam nijah paro veti ganana laghuchetasam.
Udaracharitanam the vasudhiva kutumbakam.

The feeling of my and mine will reduce. Expansion is life

contraction is death. Through, proper self-control one gets a chance to expand his awarness.

Self-Respect

Total Quality Management (TQM) places great emphasis on this quality.

A man of self-respect has clear idea of his self and is aware, at least intellectually, that the same self resides in all; hence he respects all. Self-respect gives dignity to one which should not be confused with prestige, status and privileges. Out of fullness of heart such person thinks and acts. When the glass is half empty he looks at the half that is full and strives to fill up the rest without passion. He has the conviction of the powers of goodness, he knows his strength and weakness and is not jealous of anyone better than him. He helps all who are trying to be good and do good.

Sarve yasya vinetarah, sarve pandit maninah.

Sarve mahattvamichehhanti kulam tadvasidati.

Where everyone is a *neta*, everyone is a *pandit* and all want importance whether they deserve or not, that place is destined for doom.

A man of self-respect keeps confidence in his own abilities and respects those in others, so he helps others to help himself.

He does not feel that his talents are going unnoticed and he deserves much more than what he is getting. He is wise and humble as against the creation of modern education where knowledge and arrogance goes hand in hand. Such man is clear in his habits and thought. He is obedient and at the same time independent. Above all he has dignity of labour.

Self-Effort

Many have the habit of running the show by remote control or by proxy, a very dangerous practice indeed. One who is industrious and courageous, to him comes health, wealth and prosperity; cowards talk of fate.

Udyoginam purushasimhamupaiti lakshmih daivam hi divam iti kapurusha vadanti.

Daivam nihatya pkuruouruamatmasshaktya yatne krite yadi na siddhyati koatra doshah.

Self-effort done at the right time can change future. One must exert on every detail. Timing is very important and there is no substitute for coordination of ones own faculties and others' efforts. One who listens, decides the goal with proper deliberation and then lets go the goal and concentrates on perfecting the means succeeds. The very presence of such manager inspires his co-workers. His creativity and dynamism is contagious and he commands respect and motivates everyone. Eternal vigilance is the price of liberty and alertness can be acquired through self-effort.

Excellence in work

Yogah karmasu kaushalam (*Gita*, II. 50)

A manager ought to be skilled in his work and bring out the best from himself and others. He knows that all movements are non-linear with regular ups and downs, joys and sorrows and keeps his cool under all circumstances in success and or in failure.

Samatvam yoga uchyate. (*Gita*, II. 48)

He knows however pure and fair a man be, he earns blame from others. So one must take praise and blame with equanimity.

Progressive attitude

Modern communication systems and information explosion has made the world shrink. Modern manager ought to think globally and act locally. Ruthless, indiscriminate exploitation of ecosystem has endangered even the chemistry of the air we breath. A scientific temper, combined with an intuitive futuristic vision, an idea of world situation and fast emerging socio-technical possibilities ought to be judged. A habit of study, *shravana*, deep thinking *manana* and absorption, *nididhyasana* is necessary.

Truth at any cost

Truthfulness, alignment in thought, word and deed commands respect. A will to act on decision is necessary. Openness in the management process removes suspicions and half the problems are solved.

Practice what you preach

As the great one behaves so the common man follows. The personal corporate life of a manager both inwardly and outwardly ought to be worth imitating.

As a corollary manager must face problems squarely and accept both praise and blame. The 1857 war was lost due to reluctance of the commanders to be in the forefront.

SIRADARA TO SARADARA

Itensity and pervasiveness of concern

In a family, the mother sacrifices her interest for the sake of all family members and in return gets everything. Her *tyaga* sacrifice and not exploitation earns her the unshakable position of commander of the house. She looks at members as assets to be developed and not cost to be controlled. The mother offers her services for the welfare of the whole family without expectation of returns out of her intense and pervasive concern.

CHARACTER BUILDING

Habit formation

The exercise includes giving up bad habits and building up good ones. Never talk of your faults with others but judge them and carefully remove them.

Will power is developed only through taking challenges, there is no substitute for hard work. Building up a strong good character is laborious process and patience, perseverance and purity is need to carry it out.

Value based management style is the only answer and every manager has his discretionary zone for his own experimentaion. If one changes oneself he can change his environment.

Concentration and meditation

The difference between two men is their power of concentration. Daily routine has to be set up for regular practice of concentration. At the juncture of day and night, in a clean room, on a firm seat, one should sit in a comfortable posture. After simple controlled breathing one should try to concentrate ones' mind in the region of the heart (seat of the *atman*) imagining any object like the Sun or a light. The fickle and wandering mind has to be made to sit firmly in the region of the heart. As soon as bad thoughts come good thoughts should counter them. When this concentration gets deeper, mind composes. As the day advances, through contact with others it decomposes, so it should be recomposed in the evening so that one can step into other roles in life. The

Ashtanga Yoga of Patanjali talks of *yama, niyama, asana, pranayama, pratyahara, dhyana, dharana* and *samadhi* where meditation or *dhyana* is quite a high state of absorption and composure.

Prayers

In a secular country like India prayers are a private affair and except for the National anthem all prayers are shunned in public Institutions. However, Vedic prayers offer secular and spiritual benefit and have no religious flavour.

Om saha na vavatu saha nau bhunaktu saha viryam karvaavahai Tejasvinavadhitamastu ma vidvishavahai.

Om, May *Brahman* protect us and nourish us. May we work together with great energy, may we not hate each other.

Om asato ma sad gamaya tamaso ma jyotir gamaya Mrityor ma amritam gamaya

Om From unreal lead me to the Real
From darkness to light
From death to Immortality
— *Brihadaranyaka Upa.* 1.3.28

A prayer attended by all in the corporate family ties all in a higher consciousness, creates a feeling of oneness, purifies mind and creates a holistic atmosphere through its powerful words and rythm.

Company of the enlightened

Indian ethos directed kings to take advise from men of enlightenment. *Brahmans* like Chanakya are famous for their sound advise in administration. Vidura's advise was unheeded by Dhritarashtra and he ended by losing all.

CONCLUSION

Thus we can see that ethics and morality is not blind obedience and doesn't consist in mere do's and dont's. It means making every individual acquire capacity for normal thinking and sense of freedom for taking right moral decisions after collecting all the relevant facts and weighing pros and cons of alternative decisions. Indian ethics are time tested and can introduce a new era in management for productivity and profits in the modern age.

If matter is powerful, thought is omnipotent. Bring this thought to bear upon your life, fill yourselves with the thought of your almightiness, your majesty and your glory.

14

Vivekmanagement Model

Plan for Revival of Sick units and managing organisations effectively

*Sunil Kumar**

The Chairman of Lever Brothers has identified integrity as the single most important and the one essential quality necessary in the leader.

A major problem and cause for sickness in the organisations today is that there is a total lack of trust between different people and divisions in the organisations. Unless the leaders apply *Vivekmanagement* principles and show care and concern for people and their own sincerity and integrity to the organisation and its ideals, it is difficult to win the confidence of all sections of employees.

---

* Based on the work of Vivekmanagement consultants.

Vivekmanagement is a group of professionals committed to the revival of Indian work culture based on the universal values and eternal principles epitomised in the concept of *Karma Yoga*: *Work for the realisation of divinity within oneself by serving and solving the problems of the people.*

As managers and professionals Vivekmanagement offers its services for the management and revival of the vast number of sick units in the country, based on the principle that each employee has infinite potential for perfection and the will to manifest it, in and through his work, given the suitable inspiration and an environment where he has the creativity and freedom and feels the ownership of the work he does.

SUMMARY

Symptoms of Sickness

- Fewer new ideas generation and little experimentation.
- Lack of concern for customers.
- Increase in the non-combatant to combatant ratio.
- Higher incidence of non-value adding work.
- Escalating overheads and long throughput time.
- Idle equipment resulting from tax saving investment and shrinkage of productive space.
- Procedural delays and poor house keeping.

Vivekmanagement Plan for Revival

- Move from "separatist" and "mechanistic" view of an organisation to a holistic view and bring in a more healthy concept of ownership as caretaker.
- Secure concurrence from everyone on the process of recovery.

- Form self-managing teams with specific goals and for specific tasks and ensure that they keep in touch regularly and work together in cooperation.
- Avoid routes like voluntary retirement scheme, golden handshakes and merger.

Vivekmanagement is a concept, for breakthrough improvement in productivity, quality and cost level, through step by step change in the thinking pattern of all employees which takes them from old wasteful habits to new productive ones and does away with hierarchical structure of organisation. By empowering the worker and making him think we do away with "make errors, inspect and rectify errors" of the West and replace it with zero defect of the East.

Implementation Process

- Concept learning by top management.
- Contemplation and resolving.
- Education, learning and coaching of teams.
- Loosening up by pilot projects.
- Destructuring and teaming up.
- Empowering, mobilisation and facilitation.
- Awakening to real reality.
- Visioning and management by all.

Key Concepts for Organisations

- Industry as a social system.
- Value adding, non-value adding work.
- Self-managing teams.
- Prosperity for all through productivity by all.

- Organic systems *vs.* artifical systems.
- Evolved structure *vs.* imposed structure.
- Management by all *vs.* management by few.
- 'I' centred management *vs.* 'You' centred leadership.

Key Concepts for Individuals

- Discovering divinity in Self *(Aham Brahmasmi)*
- Discovering divinity in others *(Tattvamasi)*
- Work as divine service *(yogah karmasu kaushalam)*
- Workplace as a sacred spot *(karma kshetre dharam kshetre)*
- Discovering old wasteful habits *(durguna)*
- Learning new productive habits *(sadguna).*
- Caring for others *(grahak devo bhavo)*
- Zero defect—zero breakdown—zero inventory *(Shoonya—sampoorna).*

DETAILS

Why do Organisations become Sick?

Sickness happens when people take a purely separatist and mechanistic view of the organisation, forgetting the principle of unity of existence and therefore the interconnectedness and interdependence of everything. With the separatist and mechanistic world-view, we label people and groups into impersonal sections and such separate sections do not think of the whole. We subject individuals to debilitating and often humiliating procedures and force them to undertake meaningless tasks. Alternatively, we try to buy them out with undeserved monetary compensation.

We constantly treat equal people unequally and unequal

people equally. And this causes resentments, frustrations and lack of credibility.

We never punish or reward in time and get bogged down in a plethora of rules. And this builds up mistrust and indiscipline.

As top management we keep on asking for the bottom line of profits and under such pressures for short-term immediate gains we take decisions and actions which are not good, long-term decisions. We forget the important principle that profit is an effect of long-term good decisions and actions and the money that we make from short-term gains ultimately does ruin us in the long-run.

By such acts, employees who are otherwise normal human beings, become in turn, mechanistic in their behaviour. They get set in their own titles, job description, cabins, perks and status.

Thus they become both the victims and perpetrators of an uncaring system that becomes wrapped up and goes by the name "professionalism" and passes off as 'good' management practice when it actually is anything but good.

The principles of a Healthy Organisation

Human beings are capable of thinking, planning and executing appropriate responses to developing situations.

If people are allowed to do the obvious, after being made aware of the good of the organisation then the organisation will work on its own in harmony with the rest and integrated with the environment in a mutually beneficial way.

The signs of a healthy organisation and the basic merit of a natural system is that it adapts, adjusts and accommodates itself to changing circumstances. That is the key to its survival, evolution and growth.

An organisation in which people are free to think, plan and act according to the changing circumstances survives and grows smoothly for the only reason that people adapt quickly to the dynamics of change.

And an organisation in which people are bound by inflexible job description and rigid authority structures, cannot grow for the only reason that people cannot think freely. Since everyone plans and acts without conviction the organisation becomes sick.

THE VIVEKMANAGEMENT PLAN FOR ORGANISATIONS

The Concept of Ownership

Why do people take a mechanistic view of the organisation? Because they do not have a sense of ownership of the organisation and its activities.

It is very difficult to determine who are the owners of the organisations. In many cases perhaps no one is really caring about the life and growth of the organisations. The legalistic view of ownership is that they are the shareholders, directors, trustees and the top management. This is highly limiting and does not do justice to individual motivation.

The concept of ownership needs to be looked into both practically and philosophically.

In practical terms, once a certain amount of money is invested in assets for producing goods or services, the productivity is determined by the producer. If the "legal" owner lets all producers (employees) have the feeling of ownership by giving them operational freedom, they will work towards securing maximum productivity out of the given assets.

If the 'legal owner' goes further and links their renumeration to output (in terms of factors like quantity, quality, timeliness and cost of output) then the employees will feel and work like partners.

In philosophical terms, everything belongs to one creator. None of us are permanent. We are all temporary creations of God. We do not bring anything into this world nor can we take away anything from this world. When such is the temporariness of the legal owner, why quarrel over legal ownership.

Instead let everybody, financiers, managers, trade unions, supervisors, officers, clerks, workers, salesman, suppliers and customers be the "caretakers" of the physical assets.

Let all wealth of the organisation be the "commonwealth."

If those in change of a unit can make this *metal transition from ownership to "caretakership"* the recovery of the organisation can commence from any point of its current sickness.

IMPLEMENTATION

Based on these concepts 'the steps needed for creating a shared ownership', are as follows:

First Step: Togetherness, Sharing and Caring

- To secure concurrence of all employees and concerned parties for the process of organisational recovery.
- The basic thing is to actively share the present status

of the organisation with everyone—facts and figures, concern and hopes, concepts and prescriptions.

- Talk to individuals at all levels, talk to groups, invite people to open up with their feelings, ideas and solutions.
- Ask everyone to be a caretaker. If any agreement is conditional then let these conditionalities be recorded and agreed to by all.
- Let the talks be sincere and frank exchange so that the mistrust between different sections is removed and replaced by mutual trust.

Second Step: The Concept of Self-Managing Teams

- Form voluntary teams at different levels for specific purposes.
- In the first stage volunteers can be grouped into two main streams. "Future building teams" and "Management of 'present' operations team."
- Future building teams can in turn consist of a "vision team" to think about the future and several "project team" to plan the details and execute them.
- The 'present' team can be one "guardian team," a few "facilitator teams" and several "producer teams."
- All teams are flat organisations with a "convenor" and a "reporter."

VISION TEAMS

The vision team concentrates first on stopping activities which lose money at present and which have no future.

It then moves surplus employees from existing activities to new projects, with retraining as necessary.

It formulates new project proposals based on the study of changes in customer preferences, competitor activities and new technologies.

If a company can develop 'unique' features and skills and aims at gaps in market, success is automatic.

The project team can be set up for mass training of employees, development of new products, new markets, capacity expansion, diversification, restructuring.

The guardian team undertakes the task of forming producer team and facilitator team and through them fulfilment of daily needs of internal/external customers.

The facilitator team concentrate on removing the ignorance and obstacles faced by the 'producer team.'

The producer team is encouraged to undertake continuous improvements in housekeeping, zero defect, right first time, waste identification and elimination, simplification of procedures, zero delay practices, finding out and meeting the unfulfilled needs of internal/external customers, zero breakdown practices, zero accident practices, self-performance appraisal and improvement and self-management.

The facilitator team undertakes improvement tasks such as punctuality, reduction in set up time, pull system of planning, visual controls, kit forming and processing, low cost automation.

The guardian teams undertakes improvement projects like disposal of surplus assets, finding new uses for idle land, idle plant, getting contract work, work subcontracting, devising payment by results methods, community self-help projects and inter-firm cooperative projects.

COORDINATION

Different teams coordinate and cooperate with each other through periodic meetings of convenors where they present team achievements, plans, support needed and available.

EXIT POLICIES

Popular remedies of industrial sickness like exit policy, golden handshakes, merger with healthy units are based on mechanistic view of business and can prove counter productive to the society and nation and to everyone in the long-run.

Sick units do have permanent non-decaying assets like goodwill, skills, contacts, etc. which have been built over time. All these assets can be made use of.

No voluntary retirement scheme is really voluntary and only useful people leave. If we make the industry a place for continuous learning and growing and the employees motivated and inspired to grow, then these will keep the industry young and energetic.

Why waste scarce money on golden handshakes on employees who often are the root cause of the schemes. Will such people remain useful to society after VRS or is it better to find uses for this money for collective good of the society.

Mergers are often done for taking advantage of land prices or tax laws. If the root cause of sickness is not tackled, the merger will affect the healthy unit also.

CONCLUSION

A group of eminent Management consultants like Dr. N.H. Athreya, G. Narayana and Suresh Pandit have evolved this Vivekmanagement model. By adopting these concepts many units are already on the road to recovery. These include a paper mill in U.P., Air India Loaders, MTNL operators, etc. Typically, results start showing within 3 months and a full recovery may take 12-36 months.

Similar turnaround projects are underway all over the world where the basic change is to *involve all employees in the management*. In USSR the State-owned units are now given to employees. In Spain, people owned and managed banks, manufacturing units, service centres have brought prosperity to many communities.

Unselfishness is more paying, only people have not the patience to practise it.

15

Self-Managed Teams

Suresh Pandit* on how a paper mill at Ayodhya Pioneered a New concept in 'People Involvement'

The sleepy town of Ayodhya shot into prominence in October 1990 because of the Ram Janmabhoomi Shilanyas ceremony. The curfew imposed suddenly by the Uttar Pradesh government caused severe hardship to the citizens of Ayodhya who found themselves imprisoned in their own homes for over four weeks. They were subjected to hardships of a degree that no civilised society can ever think of. However, unintentionally though, the event led to what is perhaps a unique experiment in an industrial unit in Ayodhya.

Yash Paper Mills was an agro-based, 20 tpd pulp and paper mill employing 350 persons at the time with a turnover

* A leading Management coach and facilitator who has pioneered the Vivekmanagement model.

of Rs. 4 crore. Located in the predominantly agricultural belt of Uttar Pradesh, it could attract only local people for employment. Most of the workmen were first generation employees and came from the surrounding farmland.

The founder managing director, K.K. Jhunjhunwala, came from an entrepreneural family but had no technical or formal management education. However, he was a keen learner and a self-made man who encouraged others to learn, innovate, experiment and become self-reliant.

I met him for the first time in Delhi in 1987. He was participating at of one of my intercompany programmes on quantitative and measurable goal setting. He liked the programme content and asked me if I would conduct a similar programme for his inhouse managers. He insisted however that I should conduct the programme in Hindi. I had not done so before. It was a challenge that I decided to take.

THE CURFEW

The declaration of curfew had caught the employees of Yash Paper Mills unawares, as it had the rest of the citizens of Ayodhya. While the owner, managers and officials of the mills were locked in their respective homes, the shift employees and workmen were trapped within the premises of mills located on the outskirts of the town. No telephone contact was possible between the two because the lines had gone dead. The mills had no stock of food and no one had any idea of how long they would have to starve.

Anybody would expect the workmen, under such trying circumstances, to abandon their workplaces and rush to the nearest safety zones. However, in a commendable display of bravery, the workmen of Yash Paper Mills stuck on undaunted by internal and external difficulties. Deploying commando-style operations which effectively hood-winked the curfew enforcers, they organised supplies of food and other vital items. They not only carried on like this till the curfew was officially lifted but produced record quantity of paper, of consistent quality, during the period.

THE AFTERMATH

A year later, in October 1991, K.K. Jhunjhunwala organised another visit of mine to Ayodhya. He wanted me to explore the feasibility of training workmen in 'goal setting.' It was a tall order. All the same, based on the successes scored during the earlier visits, I started talking to the groups of workmen. When I explained the concept of self-managing as a background for goal setting process, they warmed up and told me that they had already practised it. They also described their experience during the 1990 curfew.

With a combination of pain and surprise, I asked them why they did not continue the practice. They told me how things returned to 'normal' when the managers came back and took away all their authority. I asked them whether they were ready to take on the responsibility of the day-to-day running of the mill once again if I arranged for the return of the authority now resting with the managers and of course the owner. They were ready.

THE EXPERIMENT

When I talked to the owner and the managers about the formation of self-managing, self-sufficient and self-leading teams (SMTs) of employees at different levels, they were impressed with the novelty of the idea and its potential. They were apprehensive however about the long-term effects. But as we developed the concept into concrete structures, systems and staffing, they became enthusiastic.

The main features of the experiment, as discussed and agreed upon, were the following:

- The workmen and the office staff would be re-organised into multi-disciplinary 'producer teams.' Each team would be responsible for supplying one item to the next team. Each team would consist of all the persons presently engaged in the supply of that item, irrespective of their current titles or the sections or departments to which they belonged. The team would have full authority needed to fulfil the requirements of the end user of its product known as the 'customer team.' Tentatively, it was felt that a total of seven producer teams would be required: (a) Raw material supply team; (b) Pulp supply team; (c) Paper roll supply team; (d) Cut paper supply team; (e) Common production services supply team; (f) Heavy repairs team; and (g) Money and information supply team.
- Each team could select a 'Facilitator' from among the company's supervisory ranks. The facilitators in turn would form a 'Facilitator team.'
- A few managers, of just the minimum number needed to keep in touch with various teams, would form a 'Guardian team.'
- Any employee not required for the day-to-day operation of the company would form part of the 'Project team' which would be responsible for planning and execution of expansion and developmental projects.

THE START

I talked to groups of workmen, both as they came to start the shift and as they ended the shift, on three successive days. Besides explaining the concept of SMTs, these meeting were meant to gather ideas and opinions of the people. It led to finetuning of the structure, systems and staffing. At the end of each meeting, I sought and secured a formal consent of each employee for switching over to a network of SMTs from the existing hierarchical pyramidal structure.

The central theme of these talks and meetings were the following:

- Empowering self and others by discovering divinity in self (*'Aham brahmasmi'*) and in others (*'Tatwamasi'*)
- Caring for others by recognising 'them' as part of 'us' (*'Vasudhaiv Kutumbakam'* and *'Grahak devo bhava' sevadharma*)
- Recognising work as an opportunity to offer divine service (*'yogah karmasu kaushalam'*).
- Recognising mission of life as continuation of god's mission of facilitating this creation (*Isha vasyam, idam sarvam'*)
- Working for zero-erros, zero-delay, zero-wastage and zero-accidents (*'Sampoorna'* through *'Shoonya'*)
- Making the workplace sacred—cleaning, orderliness and regularity (*'Karma-kshetre'* as *'dharma-kshetre'*)

THE YIELD

- All the teams had started functioning. Work-related decisions were taken in the informal floor meeting by consensus. Formal weekly meetings of all team members were taking place regularly. The conveners were called *'Pradhans.'* The minutes of the meeting were maintained. The facilitators, also called *'Sahayaks,'* played their roles fully by providing back-up without appearing to be overbearing.

- The *sahayaks* invited the general secretary of the union, to become a 'facilitator's facilitator.' Mishra, the secretary, was touched by this vote of confidence and trust in him. He personally took the challenge of making the whole experiment successful. He spent most of his waking hours in the factory for these three months. He got a special *kutir* built for the purpose of holding formal weekly meetings and saw to it that all members took part in the meeting and contributed.
- Cleanliness drive, besides making the whole site clean, resulted in some unexpected benefits. A typical paper mill operation involves handling considerable amount of dusty material like bagasse and gunny. It also involves use of water in the process for cooling and cleaning. Most mills give up on cleaning and present a very unattractive sight. Yash Paper Mill was no exception.

The idea of preventing generation of dust and dirt, rather than getting busy later on in cleaning it up, appealed to the workmen. One by one they plugged the source of dust and dirt. For example, dust would spread throughout the mill when cut bagasse fell on the loading platform. Various suggestions emerged in the team meetings. One was to let the cut bagasse fall on another small conveyor, on the way to the digestor. This was tried successfully and dust level came down drastically. An unintended by-product of this improvement was reduction in man-hours required to push the cut bagasse into digestors. A dozen persons, who had to work with cloth masks on the faces were happy to be relieved of this back-breaking work and unhealthy surroundings. The team was not satisfied as the dry bagasse continued to spread some dust. That was when somebody came up with the idea of spraying caustic soda solution on to the smaller conveyor. This was a real breakthrough. Not only did the dust level go to zero, the consumption of caustic soda got reduced by 20 per cent and the paper quality became consistent.

- The zero-error movement also caught on. Nobody had the right to carry on with substandard operating conditions and everybody had the right to stop a wrong operating condition. This of course, resulted in reduction in production quantity in the early stage, causing anxious moments to everyone. There was always a temptation and pressure to compromise on quality for the sake of quantity.

However, the workmen withstood the pressure till the good news started trickling in from the market. Even the competitors were surprised at the sudden improvement in quality of the Yash Paper. Very soon Yash Paper started commanding a premium of Rs. 2,000 per tonne over other brands. The battle for quality was won.

THE CONSOLIDATION

- Interpersonal conflicts within the teams started appearing. This was attributed basically to the fault finding approach of most members. The trust was very much there as there was no doubting of each other's intentions. The difference of opinion was with respect to the selection of routes to the solution of problem.

The team members were given the demonstration of actual problem-solving in a classroom setting with the intervention of a facilitator. This learning exercise enabled the producer teams to appreciate and practise mutually supportive problem-solving approach.

- The union leader Mishra and another promising leader Mahavir Singh were sent to Excel Industries units in Bombay and Bhavnagar, where SMTs are in operation since inception. They came back with the awareness of widening the scope of SMTs even to the community neighbourhood. In their 45 days stay, they participated in all the activities of SMTs of Excel industries. They initiated a basic change in the dealings with surrounding villagers. Instead of the previous policy of appeasement, the Yash family members started taking active interest in solving the real problems of the surrounding villagers who in turn stopped creating problems for the mill operation.

- When the works manager, with a formal degree in paper technology and two decades of managerial experience, resigned, the facilitators took up the challenge of learning the required technology from technical consultants and producing world class paper.
- The sales people started taking the various members of the producer teams to dealers, stockists and actual users of the paper, with view to give them first hand feel of the customer requirements and commercial conditions. This exercise improved the quality response to customers and cut down the response time considerably.
- The physical custody of stores was transferred to respective producer groups. The producer teams took all the decisions regarding procurement. The members were exposed to the technical presentation by representatives of the vendors regarding their products.
- The role descriptions of producers, facilitators, guardians, conveners and reporteurs were written down and the schedule of meetings and members was documented.
- Freed of the burden of day-to-day management, the managing director could make an extensive study tour of the European mills and made concrete plans of

modernisation. He also became aware of the vast international market for agro based paper plants and developed needed contacts.

- 20 tpd unit was established to make better grade paper. Many employees from the first unit volunteered to go to the second unit and run that mill with SMTs from the first day operation.

THE ALL ROUND REVOLUTION

It has been always exciting to revisit Ayodhya. The people look forward to my visit. They have so many good news to give. Some examples:

- 25 per cent increase in the production level of the first unit.
- 50 per cent drop in broken paper in rolls which has to be recycled.
- 25 per cent reduction in electricity consumption.
  - They do face problems but none is weighed down by them. For every problem, they come up with ten solutions. There is discussion, experimentation, failure, success, learning and sharing. At the end of the day everyone goes home with a feeling of achievement and satisfaction. Everyday starts with group prayer, group meditation, sharing of good news, sharing of new learning and '*sankalp*' for the day.
  - The team members discipline themselves. Once a member was caught sleeping and everyone was unanimous in suggesting that he be marked absent for the whole shift. Problems related to work allocations, absenteeism and negligence are tackled by team members themselves.

- The union leaders sit with the guardian team members to arrive at the most equitable sharing of gains of productivity and quality improvements. These agreements have increased the earning level by 20 per cent in one year.
- A grateful managing director has decided to "gift" 400 equity shares to every employee in the forthcoming issue of the company.

If matter is powerful, thought is omnipotent. Bring this thought to bear upon your life, fill yourselves with the thought of your almightiness, your majesty and your glory.

16

Loaders of Air India: An Experiment in Motivation

Suresh Pandit and N.H. Atthreya on how the quality of worklife of 800 loaders of Air India was enriched through a motivational training programme designed by them*

Out of all the assignments that we have undertaken so far, this one appeared the least promising in the beginning. In retrospect, however, it turned out to be one of the most satisfactory experiments in terms of concrete results achieved by the participants. In fact, it was a new learning for us the trainers, wherein the educators themselves had a number of lessons to learn.

* Dr. N.H. Atthreya, Ph.D (Harvard) is a leading consultant and a Rajarishi, inspiring people for excellence.

Going by the common perception about the 'loaders,' we were wondering what good at all will come out of spending enormous amount of time and effort in educating the employees who do very 'ordinary' work. As it happened, we were in for pleasant tidings.

THE FIRST LESSONS

When Subroto Ghosal of Air India Staff College invited us to conceptualise and implement a training module for the loaders of the premier national carrier, our first reaction was sense of surprise. We were aware that Air India Staff College had one of the finest training setups of its kind in the country. The college had been training airlines personnel at all levels for decades. It had earlier trained the loaders also, particularly in handling special situations and special cargo. But Ghosal wanted something more than conventional training. Our brief was to secure a total turnabout in their attitudes towards customers. Air India wanted its loaders to care for its customers.

Quite appropriately, the first question we asked was: where did the loaders figure in the business of caring for customers.

Decades ago, the maiden contact for passengers with Air India was the well trained ground hostess sitting at the booking office. As the travel agency business gradually picked up in the country, hardly any passenger went to the airlines' own booking office to reserve his ticket. Ticketing began to be done mostly through travel agents. As a result, the ground hostess ceased to be the initial contact point. She was replaced by the loader in the departure lounge. The Air India loader became the first representative of the airlines that passengers would meet on arrival at the airport.

Inevitably, his general appearance and conduct influenced the impressions the passengers would form about the airlines as a whole and its commitment to customer service and customer care.

To put it differently, the loader was the first point of either a repeat sale or a cause of switchover to competing airline. He was one of the focal points in passenger perception about safety and efficiency of airline operations.

We also realised that , apart from the importance of the job itself, the complexity of the job of the loaders had been increasing day by day. They were required to handle such diverse cargo as live animals, radioactive materials, diplomatic mail, hazardous chemicals and electronic goods. But they were not adequately trained. While other staff members were regularly undergoing periodic training and refresher programmes, the loaders were an exception. The major problem in this regard was language. Very few loaders were conversant with English—the familiar language of all trainers.

THE ACTION RESEARCH

The first step we undertook was to observe the loaders at work, meet them and converse with them in their own language. Many aspects of their work, circumstances, relationships, beliefs, attitudes and values came to light.

Some of them were the following:

- They were very proud to be part of Air India organisation. But they were not so proud of their designation.
- They were well off materially. Most of them had gone abroad as part of their work and considered their work quite important. But they were acutely conscious of the

low status accorded to them by other staff of Air India, by their neighbours and by the society in general. Particularly painful for them was the discrimination their wards faced for being the children of 'loaders.'

- They were proficient at work. Their average experience was more than 15 years. They had many outstanding achievements to their credit. They had helped in the design and layout of Sahara cargo complex whose utilitarian features had elicited admiration from experts. Their expertise in pellet preparation was appreciated worldwide. They had been rewarded for heroic acts of rescues of passengers from crash sites. They had helped in extinguishing fires and tracing missing parcels. In a record performance during Delhi Asiad days, when over 5,000 colour TV sets had to be delivered to individual importers before the start of the games, they had worked without break for 72 hours.
- As individuals, they took considerable interest in the affairs of the community, their native villages and their neighbourhoods. Many of them from Konkan regularly sent part of their salary for the village school. A group from Himachal had started a unique scheme of hospitality. Anybody coming from their village Ganjari to Bombay got free accommodation and food in the city. They had also contributed from their salary to build a water tank and community welfare centre in their native place.
- Although their general education was low, there were many matriculates, some graduates and even one postgraduate among them. Prakash Jadhav had his book of poetry *'Dastakat'* published in 1978. His play *'Anakhi ek Hindustan'* got a state government award. Shrilochan Prasad won a Rs. 12,000 prize in a wrestling bout. He

represented Air India between 1974 and 1982 in wrestling. Fernandes had a hobby of aircraft modelling. Bir Masuvkar was a skilled die-maker. V. V. Kadam performed on stage.

- Of course, there was a high level of absenteeism among them which had caused problems at workplace. Supervisors often found them suddenly "missing" from workplaces. The absenteeism was largely due to alchoholism and the burden of bringing up large families.

THE PROGRAMME

Based on the findings of action research, we intereacted with the faculty of the Air India Staff College and the line managers and developed the outlines of the programme.

The broad strategy was:

- to raise the'self-esteem of the target group;
- to encourage them to deal with life in its totality since worklife affected homelife and *vice versa*;
- to appeal to the right brain in a holistic experiential manner rather than address to the left brain with knowledge;
- to use the medium of *'bhajan'* and *'keertan'* and of Indian languages as the medium of communication;
- to give feed-forward to supervisors and supporting group of employees and
- to give training first to a pilot group and improvise the programme as things went by.

THE TRAINING MODULES

Each participant was to be exposed to four training modules.

The first module focused on the theme of "Caring for others" in which the target group included Air India customers, their baggage, Air India cargo, family members, neighbours, relatives, community members and countrymen. A video message from the commercial manager made the start. A rendering of various '*bhajans*' by our colleague, R. P. Nadkarni, kept the participants enthralled. Particulalry effective was the *bhajan* on getting rid of bad habits. Many participants took an on-the-spot oath to give up bad habits and handed over their last cigarette pack to the trainer. The three hour module concluded with the specially composed company-song in Hindi '*Hum Air India ko chamakayenge.*'

The second three hour module focused on the theme of "Empowering self and others." It started with the discovery of divinity within oneself (*aham brahmasmi*) and in others (*tatwamasi*). The participants were invited to make inventory of 'hardware' items within them (*laxmi*) and their abilities and knowledge (*sarasvati*) and realise the power within to manage the whole universe (*govinda*). They were also made to realise the difference between 'work' and 'service' and the natural imperative of doing one's own duty (*svadharma*).

The third three-hour module dealt with the theme of 'Total productivity.' The concept of zero defect, zero delay, zero waste and zero accidents was dealt with. The relation between personal productivity and all round prosperity was established.

The fourth three-hour module dealt with the theme of 'Interpersonal relations.' The manner of how best to handle day-to-day issues in a group situation was illustrated by taking up the right way and the wrong way of going about the whole thing.

A total of about 800 employees in Bombay, Delhi, Calcutta and Madras airports were covered. The programme started in 1988 and concluded in 1990.

At the end of the programme, a sample of 300 employees was interviewed individually with a view to find out the effect the training had on their worklife and homelife.

THE RESULTS

The following are free translations of some of their quotes:

- Ready to do any work now. Previously used to choose work of my liking. Time is now better utilised. Not ashamed of being a loader. I like my work. Have become more punctual. Learnt the importance of welcoming passengers with a smile and being polite to them. I take better care of baggage and cargo. Am better dressed and neater in appearance. Increased fellow-feeling among loaders.
- Have become self-reliant. Organise and check the work on my own. Got the restroom at Delhi airport cleaned up and made it decent by a self-help plan.
- Air India is now like a second home, a school and a temple. We serve, we learn. We respect others, we get respect. We are at peace with ourselves and others. We think. We have group prayers and we feel like '*yogis*.'
- Gave up smoking and drinking. Wife and children were very happy. Saved at least Rs. 500 per month. Spent more time with children. Started helping wife in housework. Became more caring at home. Started taking interest in studies and future career building of my children.
- Resumed previously interrupted studies. Have offered to teach a language, a hobby or a vocation to others.

- Shared all this learning with family members and neighbours.

"It is good and very grand to conquer external nature, but grander still to conquer our internal nature. It is grand and good to know the laws that govern the stars and planets; it is infinitely grander and better to know the laws that govern the passions, the feelings, the will of mankind."

17

Caring for the Customer: An Experiment at MTNL

NH Atthreya and Suresh Pandit Explain how the skills of telephone operators were enhanced

When Mahanagar Telephone Nigam Limited (MTNL) was carved out of the Department of Telecommunication in 1987, it was given a clear mandate—to provide world-class service to the metropolitan subscribers of Bombay and Delhi. Even as the new organisation was meant to become an autonomous outfit with freedom from bureaucratic control, there was a rider attached to that freedom. All allocation of funds from the 'plan expenditure' account of the government of India, limited though it had been for years, were to be "frozen" and MTNL would have to raise its own funds and run on its own steam.

Evidently, the general manager of Bombay MTNL, MC

Venkatram, had his job cut out for him. He had to prioritise between several conflicting issues. In the immediate context, he had to address himself to two specific demands. On the one hand, the subscribers in the city were clamouring for more facilities and better services. On the other, funds of the tune of Rs. 300 crore required for modernisation had to be mobilised from the very same people. It was a catch 22 situation. No investments would be forthcoming unless the quality of telephone services were improved and no quality improvement was possible without adequate funding.

SUCCESSFUL INNOVATIONS

The GM thought of a median approach. He felt that if he could show some marginal improvement in the telephone services in the short run, the Bombayites, quite typically, would rise to the occasion and respond adequately to the proposed MTNL Bond Issue. He therefore decided to improve the quality of the corporation's human resources, empower the existing employees and, through them, provide better service to subscribers.

The task had to be carried within the framework of existing facilities and without any major financial burden.

He set about the task by exploring various avenues of human resources development. There was of course no dearth of professional HRD talent in Bombay. But he was "disappointed," as he told us when we met him, at the elitist approach of the specialists and their unwillingness to give any Performance Guarantee on an assignment. He was therefore impressed when in our very first meeting we broached the subject of performance parametres in order to evaluate the effect of training. He also liked the idea of 'action research' and to tailoring the training inputs based on such a research.

THE BEGINNING

MTNL was, and continues to be even today, an ocean with over one lakh employees, scores of departments and hundreds of locations. The crucial question in such a setting was: where would one begin? After considerable brainstorming, the Prabhadevi Special Services and Trunk Booking Exchange was selected. The reasons were four-fold. This particular exchange provided direct personal contact between employees and the subscribers; its facilities were relatively modern; its staff was comparatively younger, more flexible in their mindsets and more receptive to the idea of a change; and its top brass were very enthusiastic and ready and willing to take a lead in the experiment.

Incidentally, the Prabhadevi exchange catered primarily to Bombay suburbs. Special service and trunk booking calls from all local exchanges starting with digits 4, 5 and 6 also landed there. Its subscribers could get services like morning alarm (173), directory enquiries (197), assistance (199) and trunk booking (180). Around 700 telephone operators (mostly girls), about 120 supervisors (who were essentially operators promoted internally) and monitors and 25 officers provided round-the clock service at the Prabhadevi exchange.

ACTION RESEARCH

When we observed the telephone operators at work, the sheer monotony and the strain of it struck us most. The long rows of telephone boards hardly provided any moving space for the individual operator. The calls kept on coming in without interruption. Every caller assumed automatically that the telephone operator had only just woken up from a long sleep. The assumption showed in the verbal assault that often followed. In actual fact, the operator did not have time to take even a deep breath. The terminals were so close to each other that the cummulative noise "leaked" to the subscriber at the other end, giving him or her a false impression that the operators were all engaged in gossiping. The subscribers would imagine all kinds of other "crimes" on the part of the operators and work off their anger and frustration on them. As if this was not enough, there were amorous subscribers harassing the hapless girls on the line. There were many occasions when the girls could not take it any more, buckled under the sheer pressure of such harassment and broke down completely.

Besides managing this back-breaking routine at work, these girls also had to manage their homes. They had to handle unhelpful husbands, uncaring in-laws, children and meet an unending list of demands from others. They also had to come in different shifts. A number of them had to 'run' between Dadar station and Prabhadevi exchange as the distance was too short for the use of public transport and too long for a leisurely walk.

The lady supervisors played favourites. Though they were victimised in their earlier career as telephone operators, they became 'mothers-in-law' as soon as they were promoted and started victimising the telephone operators. Their only concern was 'out-turn' and they had no time or inclination to be emphathetic to the operators.

The male operators were mostly ill at ease with the all female staff. They would be either too mild and ineffective or too overbearing and counter productive.

LISTENING TO THE CUSTOMERS

We invited some frequent users among subscribers to the exchange. The purpose was to know from them first hand what improvements they expected in the services being provided by the exchange. Interaction with them was video-recorded. The response of the subscribers was open, candid and helpful. They were also taken round the exchange. One lady subscriber was so touched at the sight of conditions under which the telephone operators had to work, day in and day out, that she exclaimed: "I would never have complained against them if I had seen their plight before." The tale of torture a subscriber underwent, while waiting for the return call from the exchange after he called up 'morning alarm', led to discontinuation of the 'return call' practice. It gave immediate relief to subscribers and the out-turn also went up.

The common requirement of all customers was prompt response, courteous reply, honest reply and willingness to do all that was possible.

LISTENING TO THE TELEPHONE OPERATORS

We played the subscriber feedback on the video, incorporating a video-message from the GM, to pilot groups of telephone operators. We asked them in turn what their requirements were to fulfil the expectations of the subscribers and of the GM. The requirements of the telephone operators were recorded in the form of critical incidents and these fell in four categories:

- improvement in the behaviour of supervisors towards the telephone operators (from a 'mother-in-law' to a 'mother');
- modification in the outdated rules and practices. (A commonly cited reference was that the British India Telephone Act still applied which expected the telephone operator to reply in English even when the subscriber spoke in Indian languages and an 'erring' telephone operator was issued a memo.);

- prompt and regular maintenance of equipment and
- provision of absolutely essential and inexpensive amenities like lighting in the walk-ways, tea service at night, easy access to a doctor, etc.

IMPROVEMENT AT WORK SITE

Immediate action was initiated to set right the very obvious short coming. Lighter headsets were provided. Sound insulation between terminals was tried out. The scope of preventive maintenance was widened. Amenities were upgraded wherever it could be done within the sanctioned budget. Managers were apprised of the action research findings and were involved in developing appropriate inputs for supervisors and telephone operators.

The root cause of 'mother-in-law' behaviour of the supervisors came to light in the reactions of the pilot group. It was found that they were addressing the operators not by their names but by their staff numbers. The operators in turn addressed the supervisors as 'madam.' It was suggested that, having known each other for so many years, the operators and the supervisors could hereafter be on first name basis. This suggestion was readily accepted. There were instant scenes of reconciliation, celebration, joy and tears. The impersonal, hostile workplace had turned into a second home. The performance indicators started showing positive trend after this incident based on 'oneness'/Tatvamasi.

THE TRAINING

All the telephone operators were exposed to four training modules of 150 minutes each.

The first module was videoviewing of subscriber feed back and the GM's message to the telephone operators.

The second module centred around voice improvement exercises.

The third module gave practice in elements of transactional analysis and examined several standard expressions which would come in handy in handling different categories of subscribers like the angry subscriber, the amorous subscriber and the difficult subscriber.

The fourth module featured a video film on the correct handling of equipment in terms of do's and don'ts and the positive feedback received from subscribers and supervisors.

Supervisors received several training lessons. They were given leadership skills training, behavioural skills training and time management tips.

OBJECTIVES AND RESULTS

The conversations between operators and subscribers were 'overheard', by turn, by a 'blind' monitor. They were later rated. The number of "acceptable conversations accounted for 48 per cent of the total before the training. It meant that 52 per cent had been unacceptable. Our objective was 50 per cent improvement i.e.; 72 per cent of the total conversations should be acceptable.

The actual achieved was 96 per cent for the quarter in which training was in progress and more than 96 per cent in subsequent quarters.

In the reference period before training, billing errors amounted to 314 per quarter. An improvement of 50 per cent meant a target of 157 per quarter. What the employees actually achieved was 74 per cent per quarter during training period.

Venkatram had allowed us a fall in the out-turn of up to five per cent because five per cent of the staff would be tied up in training at any given point of time. However, thanks to the excellent cooperation of the staff of the Prabhadevi exchange, there was a record rise of 22 per cent in the number of calls. The extra revenue brought in by the additional out-turn was enough to pay for the cost of training. It also enabled MTNL to extend the training to 2,000 other telephone operators in the Fountain Exchange, Woudby Road Exchange and the International Exchange.

POST-SCRIPT

Subsequent visits to Prabhadevi exchange and reports from the managers indicate that the performance has stabilised at higher level. Training was extended to cover new comers from time to time. Suggestions have been given to maintain the spirit and enthusiasm at high level.

That which is selfish is immoral, and that which is unselfish is moral.

18

Breakthrough Through Bhakti Model

*Suresh Pandit**

Menon Pistons Ltd., Kolhapur, is a ISO-9002 company today. It celebrated its Silver Jubilee last year. It supplies pistons and rings to most of the makers of automobiles. It is the exclusive supplier of pistons for SUZUKI MARUTI's ZEN engine which is considered the most Hi-tech cars of all.

The company, founded by Menon Brothers, always took pride in quality and spared no efforts in achieving technological excellence. Their production facility at Kolhapur stands out majestically off Bombay-Bangalore Highway, amidst well maintained gardens. A visitor is at once impressed by the high level of beauty, cleanliness and order inside and outside the work-place.

---

* Courtsey, Management Ideas, N.H. Atthreya, MMC School of Management.

Ram Menon, the founder Chairman, along with his brother late Chandran Menon started the enterprise in a modest way with a unique reconditioning facility. Faced with a perpetual shortage of spare parts and taking cognisance of the high level of engineering skills and learning ability of local people, they realised the tremendous potential for engine spare parts and put up the first plant to make pistons, production of rings, pins, bearings, engine etc. followed with production facilities located in and around Kolhapur, under various group companies. Even today, Ram Menon, feels totally at home with auto-mechanics, machine operators and machine-tools. For him engineering excellence comes first, profits come incidentally.

THE SETBACK

Menon Pistons reached the zenith with supply of pistons for Soviet 'LADA' cars in 80's. It brought record turn-over and profits for the company. The earnings of employees also went up. However, the collapse of the Soviet Union and the sluggishness of the Indian economy, in the early 90's, gave the company a double blow. The company had to fight for survival. Because of the bulk orders of LADA, the company had neglected its traditional customers base of re-borers and replacement market. The management had tolerated many wasteful practices which became institutionalised, in course of time. The man power was bloated. Productivity was low and the costs were very high. There was no ceiling to the expectations of the labour for higher wages and perks. There was no dearth of leaders trying to encash on the discontent of the workmen. Inevitably, every one was talking and acting the languages of the 'force' (*Shakti*) model. Workmen had the weapon of 'with-holding work' and they started using it liberally by 'go-slow', agitations, 'work stoppages' and more restrictive practices.

The management used the weapon of with-holding money, by initiating disciplinary action, of 'issuing chargesheet', 'conducting inquiry', 'suspension' and 'dismissal.' The 'personnel professionals', 'advocates', 'labour consultants' had a field day at the expense of the company, the employees and the customers. Finally, the workmen resorted to a strike. After a prolonged strike, the workmen got exhausted and had to come back to work on terms virtually dictated by the management. Part of the agreement was guaranteed minimum output per employee with a provision of penalty for lower than guaranteed output and a production incentive for higher than guaranteed output. The guaranteed output amounted to 54,000 pistons per month.

The period after the agreement could be called as "battle of wits" between management and workmen. Management tried its best to 'extract' guaranteed production from workmen and workmen used their energy to find out some excuse or the other to lower the output. The actual output never exceeded 48,000 pistons.

RECOVERY YES, BUT

By 1994 the liberalisation measures taken by the Indian Government started having beneficial impact on the automobile industry. There was a sudden spurt in demand for engine spare parts. The company's efforts to regain the market share in replacement market also yielded good results. However, sales and profits had to be limited due to restricted output at the production stage. The financial year 1993-94 ended with sales of Rs. 2415 lakhs and profit of Rs. 70 lakhs (2.9%).

A PROMISING INDIAN MODEL

The management started looking for alternate models. Through one of the seminars attended by their HRD Manager Mr. R.S. Deshpande, they came to know about, Yash Paper experiment at Ayodhya in 'Self Managing Teams' and 'Devotional Models (Bhakti Model) of management. Mr. Deshpande instinctively felt that this could be a good way to come out of the stalemate.

The Bhakti Model is based on the Mother-Child relationship. What a mother gets is a child incapable of speaking, standing, understanding or producing. Through her selfless nurturing process, she converts the child into a responsible carpenter, architect, pilot or a doctor. Nurturing is at four levels.

- Physical nurturing—by providing food, clothing, and warmth, to make the child strong.
- Emotional nurturing—by providing encouragement, support, appreciation, to build self-confidence in the child.
- Intellectual nurturing—by providing knowledge of do's and dont's to make the child self-sufficient.
- Spiritual nurturing—by letting go the child, inspite of being deeply concerned about the welfare and safety of the child.

If the managers take on the Mother's role and give nurturing love, the child will give dedicated effort, resulting in high quality and productivity. Mr. Deshpande invited me to speak about the concept to the management and the employees representatives of Menon Pistons. Mr. Ram Menon was the first one to see the tremendous potential. The managers were impressed by the results achieved at Yash

Papers, but some had doubts whether 'Ayodhya' can be repeated at Kolhapur. Union representatives readily agreed that the 'Bhakti Model' can do wonders, but feared Menon Piston Management may not implement the concept in the right spirit. I left them for a fortnight, to contemplate over the matter.

PROVIDENTIALLY

The HRD Manager, got an opportunity to try out the new model sooner than expected, because of developments on the canteen front. The industrial canteen employing 6 workmen was run by a contractor. Because of rising prices, inadequate subsidy and low collections the contractor was compromising on quality of food; and his income fell to Rs. 700/- per day, much below the breakeven point. He couldn't pay his employees in time which made them resentful, leading to poor service. One fine morning, the contractor chose to walk-out without notice. With canteen service coming to a standstill, it was difficult to run the factory which is situated far away from the city. Mr. Deshpande had to face the music, in the absence of senior managers. To add to his woes, the six canteen workers having more than a decade of service, approached the labour commissioner claiming serverance compensation from the principal employer. The company lawyers, of course, were willing to contest the claim in courts, but could not assure Mr. Deshpande on the likely outcome. So he chose to experiment with the 'Bhakti' route.

He invited the six canteen workmen to his chambers and offered them seats, an act which they had never expected from any manager or company employee. He spoke to them as he would speak to his brothers and listened to their anxieties, complaints and hopes. All they wanted was a continuation of their regular service income, however meagre it was. Mr. Deshpande suggested them a way out. Would they like to run the canteen on their own? The first reaction was one of doubt in their own ability. Mr. Deshpande then reminded them of their own infinite human ability (*Tatvamasi*). He pointed out how they manage the organisation called home quite well (physical nurturing). He also offered whatever they wanted in organising the resources and managing the show(emotional nurturing). He asked them to make an estimate of resources they required (intellectual nurturing). They felt an initial fund of Rs. 30,000/- will be required which they could return over a period of two years assuming a sale of Rs. 1000 a day. Mr. Deshpande arranged an interest free loan from the company. He also helped them to form a formal partnership firm and got the enterprise going (spiritual nurturing). The first day sales recorded Rs. 1000. The employees were very happy with the service and the preparations. Fresh items were introduced in the menu. The second day sales rose to Rs. 1200. The canteen worker-entrepreneurs had succeeded and were confident of clearing the company loan in less than a year!

SMT BHAKTI EXPERIMENT

Meanwhile, Mr. Deshpande tried to sell the idea of self managing teams and Bhakti Model to the Hon. President of the union, Advocate P.S. Kulkarni-a staunch socialist. While Mr. Kulkarni was all for the concept, he was skeptical whether the experiment could succeed in Menon Piston, in the light of the past bitterness.

However, he was willing to keep his mind open and wished to examine at least one on going experiment personally.

Accordingly, a visit was arranged to 'Yash Paper Mills' at Ayodhya in which Mr. Kulkarni was joined by the Executive Director Mr. Mani Mathew and representatives of workmen, staff and managers. They met the *Utpadaks* (producers) *Sahayaks* (facilitators), *Sanrakshaks* (guardians) and the *Kartas* (elders). They saw the teams in action, teams in prayer meeting, teams at weekly business meetings. They witnessed how the first generation workmen took major decisions concerning every aspect of the Mill operation. They were impressed by the pride of ownership every member of 'Yash *Pariwar*' had and the total absence of the language of authority, power and status. The Kolhapur team took birth in Ayodhya and they promised me that they will create even better and more prosperous RAMRAJYA at Menon Pistons. They insisted that next time I take the visitors to Kolhapur instead of to Ayodhya!

The SMT Bhakti experiment started in the ring division from 16th May, 94 as its Manager Mr. Ramdas and his team were first to volunteer unanimously for the experiment. The division had also recorded losses (13%). All the employees of the division were given the basic understanding of the new way of industrial life, with the following concepts:

- We are born to serve others, success and prosperity come to those who perform their sacred duty (*dharma*) towards customers (*grahaks*).
- Every human being is a creator (*Brahman*) in the mould of creator (*Brahman*). Men's creative work begins where God's creative work ends.
- Wasteless, delayless, errorless, and accidentless poduction is our Yoga (joining God).
- Harmony is a natural state in the universe when every

one performs his sacred duty and does not operate from the concept of rights.

- The future we create is the only future that we share.

Natural teams of producers, facilitators, and guardians were formed.

They set their own goals, made their own plans and executed them.

The goals were set in terms of what the customers wanted. The focus got shifted from mere 'number of rings' to 'number of completed sets.'

BREAKTHROUGH

The first month of September 1994 produced a record output, 27% more than the average of earlier six months. When I asked the members the secret of their succes, they said with pride:

- There was no tension or strain of meeting management set target. The ouput came naturally by team work.
- Earlier, we were happy when machines broke down because it meant a long respite from work. This time we did not allow any machine to break down. We took good care of them.
- Everyone made sure that no defective pieces went past him. This avoided rework at later stages.
- Many small improvements were made by ourselves, without asking anybody's permission.
- We saw to it that the key machines were used to the maximum.

The management wanted to share the gains of higher productivity with workmen. A simple concept of evaluating productivity was evolved. It was P/E ratio. P was the value of production in rupees and E the total earnings of employees in rupees. If the ratio improved by 27% over base line, the members stood to gain a fixed amount approximately equal to 13.5% of their earnings.

BELIEVE IT OR NOT

The three years previous agreement between management and union was to end in March 1995. Based on the experience and mutual trust gained in the Ring Division experiment, it was decided to conduct the negotiations for the new agreement, in an atmosphere of goodwill and 'offer and accept' mode rather than 'demand and yield' mode. A negotiation was initiated, ground rules were agreed upon and satisfactory agreement was reached by May 1995. The notable aspect of the process was that the piston division achieved a record production of 60,000 pistons in March when the negotiations were on.

Even this record was broken in May 1995, with a production of 74,000 pistons, when the agreement was signed. The company ended F.Y. 1994-95 with a sale of 3373 lacs (40% growth) and Rs. 238 lacs profit before tax (24%) increase. This came at a time when the company was making plans to go public. It was a great morale booster for everyone connected with the company. 'The Menon Piston Pariwar' is confident of taking their pistons to the land of their origin Germany, UK and USA. The teams from Mercedes Benz, General Motors and Cummins have already visited the facility and are impressed by the workmanship. This is just a beginning of a new dawn for Menon Piston Pariwar.

Summing Up

Because of its spirituality, long term and Holistic vision, Indian thought has made a tremendous contribution to the world over thousands of years. Today, for some reasons India is no longer in the fore-front and the people seem to have lost pride in being Indians, forgetting the history of India as a land of wealth, prosperity and spirituality, to which have flocked people from all over the world, to partake in its glory.

It is time that our educationists, corporate leaders, managers and HRD experts draw upon the wisdom of India which has a tremendous contribution to make in the fields of education, HRD, behavioural sciences, development of mind, Management, etc. This can help us in evolving systems and structures which not only produce effective results but are also conducive to our growth towards infinite perfection and joy in-and-through our daily work. We will then catapult India once again to the pinnacle in the field of Management, HRD and Business as in the field of spirituality.